AZUSA
Street

AZUSA Street

Frank Bartleman

Whitaker House

Unless otherwise indicated, all Scripture quotations are from the *King James Version* of the Holy Bible.

Scripture quotations marked (RSV) are from the *Revised Standard Version Common Bible* © 1973, by the Division of Christian Education of the National Council of Churches of Christ in the U.S.A. Used by permission.

AZUSA STREET

ISBN: 0-88368-638-4
Printed in the United States of America
Copyright © 1982 by Whitaker House

Whitaker House
30 Hunt Valley Circle
New Kensington, PA 15068

Library of Congress Cataloging-in-Publication Data

Bartleman, Frank, 1871–1935.
  [Another wave rolls in]
  Azusa Street / by Frank Bartleman.
    p. cm.
Originally published: Another wave rolls in. Northridge, Calif. : Voice Christian Publications, 1962.
  ISBN 0-88368-638-4
  1. Bartleman, Frank, 1871-1935. 2. Pentecostals—United States—Biography. 3. Pentecostalism—United States—History—20th century.
4. Revivals—California—Los Angeles—History—20th century. 5. Los Angeles (Calif.)—Church history—20th century. I. Title.
  BX8762.Z8 B37   2000
  289.9'4'092—dc21   00-010960

1 2 3 4 5 6 7 8 9 10 11 12 13 / 07 06 05 04 03 02 01 00

Contents

Chapter 1

Beginnings

I arrived in Los Angeles, California, with my wife and two young daughters, on December 22, 1904. Little Esther, our oldest child, three years old, was seized with convulsions and passed away to be with Jesus on January 7, at 4 A.M. Little "Queen Esther" seemed to have been born *for such a time as this* (Esther 4:14).

Beside that little coffin, with heart bleeding, I pledged my life anew for God's service. In the presence of death, how real eternal issues become. I promised the rest of my life should be spent wholly for Him. He made a fresh covenant with me. I then begged Him to open a door of service quickly, so that I might not find time for sorrow.

Just one week after little Esther's departure, I began preaching twice a day at the Peniel Mission in Pasadena. While souls were saved during the month's meetings in Peniel Mission, the greatest victory gained was the spiritual growth of a company of young men attending there. A number were called out by the Lord for future service.

On April 8, I heard F. B. Meyer, from London, preach. He described the great revival then going on in Wales, which he had just visited. He had met Evan Roberts. My soul was stirred to its depths, having read of this revival shortly before. I then and there promised God He should have full right of way with me, if He could use me.

I distributed tracts in the post office, banks, and public buildings in Los Angeles and also took tracts to many saloons. Later I visited about thirty saloons in Los Angeles again. The houses of prostitution were wide open at that time, and I gave out many tracts there.

Little Esther's death had broken my heart, and I felt I could live only while in God's service. I longed to know Him in a more real way and to see the work of God go forth in power. A great burden and cry came in my heart for a mighty revival. He was preparing me for renewed service for Him. This could be brought about only by the realization of a deeper need in my own heart for God, and a real soul travail for the work of God. This He gave me. Many were being similarly prepared at this time in different parts of the world. The Lord was preparing to visit and deliver His people once more. Intercessors were the need. *"He... wondered that there was no intercessor"* (Isaiah 59:16). *"I sought for a man...[to] stand in the gap before me for the land, that I should not destroy it; but I found none"* (Ezekiel 22:30).

8

About the first of May, a powerful revival broke out in the Lake Avenue Methodist Episcopal Church in Pasadena. Most of the young men who had come forth in the meetings in Peniel Mission attended this church. They had gotten under the burden for a revival there. In fact, we had been praying for a sweeping revival for Pasadena, and God was answering our prayers. I found a wonderful work of the Spirit going on at Lake Avenue. There was no big preacher there, yet the altar was full of seeking souls. One night nearly every unsaved soul in the house was saved. It was a clean sweep for God. Conviction was mightily upon the people. In two weeks' time two hundred souls knelt at the altar seeking the Lord. The Peniel boys were involved and wonderfully used by God. We then began to pray for an outpouring of the Spirit for Los Angeles and the whole of southern California.

I find the following observations in my diary, written at that time:

> Some churches are going to be surprised to find God passing them by. He will work in channels where they will yield to Him. They must humble themselves for Him to come. We are crying, "Pasadena for God!" Some people are too well satisfied with their own goodness. They have little faith or interest for the salvation of others. God will humble them by passing them by. The Spirit is breathing prayer through us for a mighty, general outpouring. Great things are coming. We are asking largely, that our joy may be full. God is moving. We are praying for the churches and their pastors. The Lord will visit those willing to yield to Him.

And the same is true today. Ultimate failure or success for God will be realized just at this point. We must keep humble and little in our own eyes. Let us get built up by a sense of our own importance and we are gone. History repeats itself in this connection. God has always sought a humble people. He can use no other. Martin Luther, the great reformer, wrote,

> When our Lord and Master Jesus Christ says repent, He means that the whole life of believers on earth should be a constant and perpetual repentance. Repentance and sorrow— i.e., true repentance—endure as long as a man is displeased with himself. The desire of self-justification is the cause of all the distresses of the heart.

There is always much need of heart preparation, in humility and separation, before God can consistently come. The depth of any revival will be determined exactly by the spirit of repentance that is obtained. In fact, this is the key to every true revival born of God.

On May 12, God dealt with me about giving all my time to Him, turning my back finally and for all time on secular employment. He wanted me now to trust Him fully for myself and my family. I had just received a book, *The Great Revival in Wales,* written by S. B. Shaw. Taking a little walk before breakfast, I was reading this. The Lord had been trying for years to bring me to this decision for His service. We entered into a new contract between us. He was to have the rest of my life fully. And I have never dared to break this contract.

My wife kept my breakfast for me. But I did not return until noon. I had lost my appetite for food. The

Spirit, through the book, set me on fire. I visited and prayed with three preachers and a number of workers before I returned home at noon. I had received a new commission and anointing. My burden was for revival.

I visited and prayed with people all day long for some time now, distributing G. Campbell Morgan's pamphlet on the "Revival in Wales." It moved the people strongly. The spirit of prayer was increasing upon me, and I determined to be obedient to *"the heavenly vision"* (Acts 26:19). I prayed the Lord for faith to trust Him fully. *"Man shall not live by bread alone"* (Matthew 4:4).

The Lord blessed me with a further spirit of exhortation to revival among the churches, giving me articles to write for the Holiness press along the same line also. I began to write particularly for the *Way of Faith* and *God's Revivalist*. One night I awoke from my sleep shouting the praises of God. He was getting hold of me more and more. I was now going day and night, exhorting my fellowman to faith in God for mighty things. The spirit of revival consumed me. The spirit of prophecy came upon me strongly also. I seemed to receive a definite "gift of faith" for revival. We were evidently in the beginning of wonderful days to come, and I prophesied continually of a mighty outpouring.

I had a real ministry to the religious press and began to attend prayer meetings at the various churches to exhort them. G. Campbell Morgan's tract on the "Revival in Wales" spread the fire in the churches wonderfully. I did a great deal of visiting among the saints also and began to sell S. B. Shaw's book, *The Great Revival in Wales,* among the churches. God wonderfully used it to promote faith for a revival spirit. My tract work was continued among the saloons and business houses.

In May 1905, I wrote in an article,

> My soul is on fire as I read of the glorious work of grace in Wales. The "seven thousand" in the land, who have kept company with the "spared ones" (Ezekiel 9), and who have been "crying and sighing" because of the abomination and desolation in the land, the decay of vital piety in the body of Christ, may well be excused for rejoicing at such a time and prospect as this, when God is once more moving in the earth. But where are the men who will "stir themselves up to take hold of God?" Let our watchword at this time be "California for Christ." God is looking for workers, channels, worms of the dust. Remember, He must have worms. Jesus' life was pressed out in prayer at every pore. This kind comes too high for most people. But may not this be our Lord's "last call"?

On June 17, I went to Los Angeles to attend a meeting at the First Baptist Church. They were waiting on God for an outpouring of the Spirit there. Their pastor, Joseph Smale, had just returned from Wales. He had been in touch with the revival and Evan Roberts, and was on fire to have the same visitation and blessing come to his own church in Los Angeles. I found this meeting in accordance with my own vision, burden, and desire, so I spent two hours in the church in prayer before the evening service. Meetings were being held every day and night there, and God was present.

One afternoon I started the meeting in Los Angeles while they were waiting for Smale to appear. I exhorted them not to wait for man but to expect from God. They were depending on some great one, the same spirit of idolatry that has cursed the church and hindered God in all ages. Like the children of Israel, the people must have "some other god before Him." (See Exodus 20:3.) In state church circles in Europe, the pastor is often known as "the little God." I started the service in the evening on the church steps, outside, while we were waiting for the janitor to arrive with the key. We had a season of prayer for the surrounding community. The evening meeting was a steady sweep of victory.

When God's church becomes what it should be, in love and unity, the doors will never be closed or locked. Like the temple of old, it will always be open. (We saw this later, at Azusa Mission.) God does not have many churches, all of different names. There is no division in a true Pentecost or in true worship. *"God is a Spirit; and they that worship him must worship him in spirit and in truth"* (John 4:24). *"For by one Spirit are we all baptized into one body...and have been all made to drink into one Spirit"* (1 Corinthians 12:13). Ancient Israel, when right with God, was one; how much more should the church be. We have priests enough to serve continually, and plenty of seeking, needy people to fill the church at all times. How far we have fallen from the early pattern, and even from the type of the church, Israel. We are so far from it that we scarcely recognize the real thing. Even the Catholic Church, though formal, is ahead of us in this. The difficulty and shame is that we are hopelessly divided.

I went to Lamanda Park and, after preaching, spent the night at the parsonage praying and sleeping alternately. I wanted a fuller revelation of Jesus to my own soul. Like the full moon that draws clearer and nearer to our vision as we continue to steadfastly gaze at it, so Jesus appears more real to our souls as we continue to contemplate Him. We need a closer, personal, vital relationship, acquaintance, and communion with God. Only the man who lives in fellowship with divine reality can be used to call the people to God.

I went to Smale's church again, and again found them listlessly waiting for the preacher to appear. Many did not seem to have any definite idea of why they had come to the meeting. I began to pray aloud, and the meeting started off with power. It was in full blast when Brother Smale arrived. God wanted the people to look to Him, and not to man. Those not having the glory of God first in view would naturally resent this. But it is God's plan.

I found most Christians did not want to take on a burden of prayer. It was too hard on the flesh. I was carrying this burden now in ever increasing volume, night and day. The ministry was intense. It was *"the fellowship of His sufferings"* (Philippians 3:10), a *"travail"* of soul (Isaiah 53:11), with *"groanings which* [could not] *be uttered"* (Romans 8:26). Most believers find it easier to criticize than to pray.

One day I was much burdened in prayer. I went to Brother Manley's tent and fell at the altar, there unburdening my soul. A worker ran in from a side tent and begged me to pray for him. I attended another meeting that night and there found a young brother,

Edward Boehmer, who had come forth in the Peniel meetings in the spring, with the same burden of prayer on him. We were wonderfully united in the Spirit from that time on. He was destined to become my prayer helper in the future. We prayed together at the little Peniel Mission until 2 A.M. God wonderfully met and assured us as we wrestled with Him for the outpouring of His Spirit upon the people. My life was by this time literally swallowed up in prayer. I was praying day and night.

I wrote more articles for the religious press, exhorting the saints to prayer, and went to Smale's again in Los Angeles. Here I found the people waiting for the preacher again. I was greatly burdened for the situation and tried to show them they must expect from God. Some resented this, being bound by age-old custom, but others responded to it. They were praying for a revival like they had in Wales. This was one of the outstanding features there. In Wales they expected from God. The meetings went on whether the preacher was present or absent. They came to meet God. He met them.

I had written a letter to Evan Roberts in Wales, asking them to pray for us in California. I now received a reply that they were doing so, which linked us up with the revival there. The letter read as follows:

> My dear brother in the faith: Many thanks for your kind letter. I am impressed by your sincerity and honesty of purpose. Congregate the people together who are willing to make a total surrender. Pray and wait. Believe God's promises. Hold daily meetings. May God bless you, is my earnest prayer. Yours in Christ
> —Evan Roberts

We were much encouraged to know that they were praying for us in Wales.

I wrote some articles for the *Way of Faith,* the *Christian Harvester,* and *God's Revivalist* at this time. The following are extracts:

> A wonderful work of the Spirit has broken out here in Los Angeles, California, preceded by a deep preparatory work of prayer and expectation. Conviction is rapidly spreading among the people, and they are rallying from all over the city to the meetings at Pastor Smale's church. Already these meetings are beginning to "run themselves." Souls are being saved all over the house, while the meeting sweeps on unguided by human hands. The tide is rising rapidly, and we are anticipating wonderful things. Soul travail is becoming an important feature of the work, and we are being swept away beyond sectarian barriers. The fear of God is coming upon the people, a very spirit of burning. Sunday night the meeting ran on until the small hours of the next morning. Pastor Smale is prophesying of wonderful things to come. He prophesies the speedy return of the apostolic gifts to the church. Los Angeles is a veritable Jerusalem. Just the place for a mighty work of God to begin. I have been expecting just such a display of divine power for some time. Have felt it might break out at any hour. Also that it was liable to come where least expected, that God might get the glory. Pray for a Pentecost.
>
> —June 1905

One evening, July 3, I felt strongly impressed to go to the little Peniel Hall in Pasadena to pray. There I found Brother Boehmer ahead of me. He had also been led by God to the hall. We prayed for a spirit of revival for Pasadena until the burden became nearly unbearable. I cried out like a woman in birth pangs. The Spirit was interceding through us. Finally, the burden left us. After a little time of quiet waiting, a great calm settled down upon us. Then, suddenly, the Lord Jesus revealed Himself to us. He seemed to stand directly between us, so close we could have reached out our hands and touched Him. But we did not dare to move. I could not even look. In fact, I seemed all spirit. His presence seemed more real, if possible, than if I could have seen and touched Him naturally. I forgot I had eyes or ears; my spirit recognized Him. A heaven of divine love filled and thrilled my soul. Burning fire went through me. In fact, my whole being seemed to flow down before Him, like wax before the fire. I lost all consciousness of time or space, being conscious only of His wonderful presence. I worshipped at His feet. It seemed a veritable Mount of Transfiguration. I was lost in the pure Spirit.

For some time He remained with us. Then, slowly, He withdrew His presence. We would have been there yet had He not withdrawn. I could not doubt His reality after that experience. Brother Boehmer experienced largely the same thing. We had lost all consciousness of each other's presence while He remained with us. We were almost afraid to speak or breathe when we came back to our surroundings. The Lord had said nothing to us, but only overwhelmed our spirits by His presence. He had come to strengthen and assure us for His service. We knew now we were workers with Him, fellowshippers of His sufferings, in the ministry of "soul travail." Real soul travail is just as definite in the spirit as natural human birth pangs. The simile is almost perfect. No soul is ever born without this. All true revivals of salvation come this way.

The sun was up the next morning before we left the hall. But the night had seemed but half an hour. The presence of God eliminates all sense of time. With Him all is eternity. It is "eternal life." God knows no time. This element is lost in heaven. This is the secret of time appearing to pass so swiftly in all nights of real prayer. Time is superseded. The element of eternity is there. For days that marvelous presence seemed to walk by my side. The Lord Jesus was so real. I could scarcely take up with human conversation again. It seemed so crude and empty. Human spirits seemed so harsh, earthly fellowship a torment. How far we are naturally from the gentle Spirit of Christ!

I spent the following day in prayer, going to Smale's church in the evening, where I had a ministry in intercession. Heavenly peace and joy filled my soul. Jesus was so real. Doubts and fears cannot abide in His presence.

I wrote a number of articles to several papers, describing God's operations among us, and exhorting the saints everywhere to faith and prayer for a revival. The Lord used these articles greatly to bring faith and conviction. I was soon receiving quite a large correspondence from many places.

I wrote in my diary at this time the following observations:

> We may cut ourselves off from God by our spiritual pride, while He may cause the weakest to repent and go through to victory. The work in

our own hearts must go deeper than we have ever experienced, deep enough to destroy sectarian prejudice, party spirit, and so on, on all sides. God can perfect those whom He chooses.

The present worldwide revival was rocked in the cradle of little Wales. It was brought up in India, becoming full-grown in Los Angeles later. I received from God early in 1905 the following keynote to revival: "The depth of revival will be determined exactly by the depth of the spirit of repentance." And this will hold true for all people, at all times.

The revival spirit at Brother Smale's rapidly spread its interest over the whole city, among the spiritual people. Workers were coming in from all parts, from various affiliations, uniting their prayers with us for a general outpouring. The circle of interest widened rapidly. We were now praying for California, for the nation, and also for a worldwide revival. The spirit of prophecy began to work among us for mighty things on a large scale. Someone sent me five thousand pamphlets on "The Revival in Wales." These I distributed among the churches. They had a wonderful quickening influence.

I visited Smale's church again and started the meeting. He had not yet arrived. The meetings were getting wonderful by this time for their spontaneity. Our little Gideon's band* was marching on to certain

---

* When Gideon was commissioned by God to fight against the Midianites, who had invaded the land of Israel, Gideon's army consisted of only 300 men. The Midianites and their allies numbered about 135,000. Yet by God's power the small army of 300 was able to throw the enemy into complete confusion and ultimately win. (See Judges 6–8.)

victory, led by the Captain of our salvation, Jesus. I was led to pray at this early date especially for faith, discernment of spirits, healing, and prophecy. I felt I needed more wisdom and love, also. I seemed to receive a real gift of faith for the revival at this time, with a spirit of prophecy to the same end, and began to prophesy of mighty things to come.

When we began to pray in the spring of 1905, no one seemed to have much faith for anything out of the ordinary. Pessimism in regard to the then present conditions seemed to be felt generally among the saints. But this attitude had changed. God Himself had given us faith for better things. There had been nothing in sight to stimulate us to this. It came from nothing. And can He not do the same today?

I wrote an article at this time for the *Daily News* of Pasadena, describing what I saw in Brother Smale's church. It was published, and the manager himself came to see soon after. He was greatly convicted, came to the altar, and sought God earnestly. The article was copied in a number of Holiness papers throughout the country. It was entitled, "What I Saw in a Los Angeles Church." The following are some extracts:

> For some weeks special services have been held in the First Baptist Church, Los Angeles. Pastor Smale had returned from Wales, where he was in touch with Evan Roberts and the revival. He registers his conviction that Los Angeles will soon be shaken by the mighty power of God.

> The service of which I am writing began in an impromptu and spontaneous way some time before the pastor arrived. A handful of people

had gathered early, which seemed to be sufficient for the Spirit's operation. The meeting started. Their expectation was from God. God was there, the people were there, and, by the time the pastor arrived, the meeting was in full swing. Pastor Smale dropped into his place, but no one seemed to pay any special attention to him. Their minds were on God. No one seemed to get in another's way, although the congregation represented many religious bodies. All seemed to be in perfect harmony. The Spirit was leading.

The pastor arose, read a portion of the Scripture, made a few well-chosen remarks full of hope and inspiration for the occasion, and the meeting passed again from his hands. The people took it up and went on as before. Testimony, prayer, and praise were intermingled throughout the service. The meeting seemed to run itself as far as human guidance was concerned. The pastor was one of them. If one is at all impressionable religiously, he must feel in such an atmosphere that something wonderful and imminent is about to take place. Some mysterious, mighty upheaval in the spiritual world is evidently at our doors. The meeting gives one a feeling of "heaven on earth," with an assurance that the supernatural exists, and that in a very real sense.

I wrote another article for the *Wesleyan Methodist* at the same time, of which the following are extracts:

Mercy rejected means judgment, and on a corresponding scale. In all the history of God's world, there has always been first the offer of divine mercy, then judgment following. The prophets ceased not day and night to faithfully warn Israel, but their tears and entreaties for the most part proved in vain. The awful destruction of Jerusalem, in 70 A.D., which resulted in the extermination of a million Jews and the captivity of multitudes more, was preceded by the offer of divine mercy at the hands of the Son of God Himself.

In 1859 a great revival wave visited our country, sweeping a half million souls into the fountain of salvation. Immediately the terrible carnage of 1861–1865 followed. And so, as we anticipate the coming revival, which is already rapidly assuming worldwide proportions, we wonder if judgment will follow mercy, as at other times. And judgment in proportion to the mercy extended. —July 1905

For *God's Revivalist* I wrote,

Unbelief of every form has come in upon us like a flood. But lo, our God comes also! A standard is being raised against the Enemy. The Lord is choosing out His workers. This is a time to realize the vision for service. *"The LORD...hath spoken, and called the earth from the rising of the sun unto the going down thereof....Our God shall come, and shall not keep silence....Gather my saints together unto me, those that have made a covenant with me by sacrifice"* (Psalm 50:1, 3, 5).

I often used to declare during 1905 that I would rather live six months at that time than fifty years of ordinary time. It was a day of the beginning of great things. The grain of corn was willing to "fall into the ground and die" (see John 12:24), and there was promise of abundant harvest. But for spiritual "flappers,"* the whole matter was naturally foolishness.

I wrote another letter to Evan Roberts, asking for continued prayer for California. Thus we were kept linked up in prayer with Wales for the revival. In those days, real prayer was little understood. It was hard to find a quiet place where one would not be disturbed. Gethsemane experiences with Jesus were rare among the saints in those days.

At Smale's church one day, I was groaning in prayer at the altar. The spirit of intercession was upon me. A brother rebuked me severely. He did not understand it. The flesh naturally shrinks from such ordeals. The "groans" are no more popular in most churches than is a woman in birth pangs in the home. Soul travail does not make pleasant company for selfish worldlings. But we cannot have souls reborn without it. Childbearing is anything but a popular exercise, and so with a real revival of newborn souls in the churches. Modern society has little place for a childbearing mother. They prefer society "flappers." And so with the churches regarding soul travail. There is little burden for souls. Men run from the groans of a woman in travail of birth. And so the church desires no "groans" today. She is too busy enjoying herself.

We were much pressed financially again, but the Lord delivered. We never made our wants known to

---

* Flappers were young women around the time of World War I and the following decade who balked at the conventions of society and were generally considered capricious and even rebellious.

anyone but God, and we never begged or borrowed, no matter how pressing the need might seem to be. We believed that if the saints were living closely enough to God, He would speak to them. We trusted Him fully, and went without if He did not send help. I wrote my first tract at this time. It was entitled, "Love Never Faileth." This was the beginning of a large faith tract ministry. I had to trust the Lord for the means, but He never failed me.

A friend paid our expenses at a camp meeting in the Arroyo for a few days, so we tented there. It was midsummer, and we enjoyed the change and outing. I spent most of my time on my face in the woods in prayer. In the moonlit evenings, I poured out my soul unto God, and He met me there. There was much "empty wagon" rattle in the camp. Most were seeking selfish blessings. They rushed to meetings, like a big sponge, to get more blessing. They needed stepping on.

I found my soul crying out for God far beyond the seeming aspirations of most of the Holiness people. I wanted to go deeper, beneath the mere emotional realm to something more substantial and lasting that would put a rock in my soul. I was tired of so much froth and foam, so much religious ranting and pretension. And the Lord did not disappoint me.

The camp meeting committee got me on the carpet because of the tracts I was distributing in the camp. They thought I was attacking the Holiness movement, but I was only exhorting them to a deeper place in God. They needed more humility and love. My tract against sectarianism, "That They All May Be One," stirred the camp. Surely man-made movements need to be stirred. God has but one "movement"—that is His "one body." This was the message at Azusa Mission in the beginning.

I received a second letter from Evan Roberts that read as follows:

> Loughor, Wales, July 8, 1905
>
> Dear brother: I am very thankful to you for your thoughtful kindness. I was exceedingly pleased to learn the good news of how you are beginning to experience wonderful things. Praying God to continue to bless you, and with many thanks repeated for your good wishes, I am yours in the service.   —Evan Roberts

I went to Smale's church one night, and he resigned. The meetings had run daily in the First Baptist Church for fifteen weeks. It was now September. The officials of the church were tired of the innovation and wanted to return to the old order. He was told to either stop the revival or get out. He wisely chose the latter. But what an awful position for a church to take—to throw God out! In this same way, they later drove the Spirit of God out of the churches in Wales. They tired of His presence, desiring to return to the old, cold ecclesiastical order. How blind men are! The most spiritual of Pastor Smale's members naturally followed him, with a nucleus of other workers who had gathered to him from other sources during the revival. They immediately contemplated organizing a New Testament church.

I had a feeling that, at least for a time, perhaps the Lord was cutting Brother Smale loose for the evangelistic field to spread the fire in other places. But he did not see it so. I had a conference with him, with this objective in view, and was able to arrange for him to speak at the Lake Avenue Methodist Episcopal Church in Pasadena. This had been the storm center of the revival there.

The night before Brother Smale's services at Lake Avenue Church, two of us spent the night until after midnight in prayer. Brother Smale preached twice on Sunday. He was wonderfully anointed by God for the occasion. We spent the time between the services in prayer. His message was on the revival in Wales, and the people were greatly moved.

Brother Smale soon organized a New Testament church. I became a charter member, as I felt I ought to stay with them, though I did not care very much for organization. He rented Burbank Hall and prepared to hold meetings there. In the meantime, I secured the Fourth Street Holiness Hall for him, until Burbank Hall was ready.

The Lord gave me another tract, entitled "Pray! Pray! Pray!" I took it to the printer in faith, and God sent the money on time. It was a strong exhortation to prayer. Like the prophets of old, we must pray for those who will not pray for themselves. We must confess the sins of the people for them.

About this time, while Brother Boehmer and I prayed, the Spirit was poured out in a wonderful way in several meetings we were praying for. We felt we had hold of God for them. The reports proved our convictions. Prayer changes things. There is wonderful power in the proper kind of prayer. For instance, Elijah on Mount Carmel, a man of *"like passions"* with us (James 5:17). *"The effectual fervent prayer of a righteous man availeth much"* (verse 16). Confession may also be necessary in this connection. *"Confess your faults one to another"* (verse 16).

Almost every day in Los Angeles found me engaged in personal work, tract distribution, prayer, or preaching in some meeting. I was writing articles for the religious press continually. At one tent meeting in Pasadena, the Lord wonderfully anointed me in preaching, and twenty souls came to the altar. By this time the spirit of intercession had so possessed me that I prayed almost day and night. I fasted much also, until my wife almost despaired of my life at times. The sorrows of my Lord had gripped me. I was in Gethsemane with Him. The *"travail of his soul"* (Isaiah 53:11) had fallen in a measure on me. At times I feared that I might not live to realize the answer to my prayers and tears for the revival. But He assured me, sending more than one angel to strengthen me. I felt I was realizing a little of what Paul meant about "filling up the cup of His sufferings" (see Colossians 1:24) for a lost world. Some were even afraid that I was losing my mind. They could not understand my tremendous concern. Nor can very many understand these things today. *"The natural man receiveth not the things of the Spirit of God: for they are foolishness unto him"* (1 Corinthians 2:14). Selfish spirits can never understand sacrifice. But *"whosoever will save his life shall lose it"* (Matthew 16:25). *"Except a corn of wheat fall into the ground and die, it abideth alone: but if it die, it bringeth forth much fruit"* (John 12:24). Our Lord was *"a man of sorrows"* (Isaiah 53:3) as well as of joy.

I frequently went to Pasadena having to trust God for carfare to get home. On one occasion, Brother

Boehmer had an impression I was coming. He went to the little Peniel Mission and found me there. We spent several hours in prayer; then he paid my carfare home. We often spent whole nights together in prayer during those days. It seemed a great privilege to spend a whole night with the Lord. He drew so near. We never seemed to get weary on such occasions.

Boehmer worked at gardening. I never asked him for a penny, but he always gave me something. God finally got not only his money, but also his life, in His service. He was a wonderful man of prayer. God taught us what it means to *"know...no man after the flesh"* (2 Corinthians 5:16). He lifted us into such a high relationship that our fellowship seemed only in the Spirit. Beyond that we died to one another.

I wrote Evan Roberts a third time to have them continue to pray for us in Wales. In those days, after I had preached, I generally called the saints to their knees, and we would be in prayer for hours before we could get up. The Lord led me to write many leaders throughout the country to pray for revival. The spirit of prayer was growing continually.

The New Testament Church, begun by Brother Smale, seemed to be losing the spirit of prayer as they increased their organization. They now tried to shift this ministry on a few of us. I knew God was not pleased with that and became much burdened for them. They had taken on too many secondary interests. It began to look as though the Lord would have to find another body. My hopes had been high for this particular company of people, but the Enemy seemed to be sidetracking them, or at least leading them to miss God's best. They were now even attempting to organize prayer—an impossible thing. Prayer is spontaneous. I felt it were better not to have organized than to lose the ministry of prayer and spirit of revival as a body. It was for this they had been called in the beginning.

They had become ambitious for a church and organization. It seemed hard to them not to be "like the other nations (churches) round about them." (See Deuteronomy 17:14.) And right here they began to fail. As church work increased, they lost sight of the real issue. Human organization and human programs leave very little room for the free Spirit of God. It means much to be willing to be considered a failure, while we seek to build up a purely spiritual kingdom. God's kingdom *"cometh not with observation"* (Luke 17:20). It is very easy to choose second best. The prayer life is needed much more than buildings or organizations. These are often a substitute for the other. Souls are born into the kingdom only through prayer.

I feared the New Testament Church might develop a party (sectarian) spirit. A rich lady offered them the money to build a church edifice. The Devil was bidding high. However, she soon withdrew her offer, and I confess I was glad she did. They would soon have had no time for anything but building. It would have been the end of their revival. We had been called out to evangelize Los Angeles, not to build up another sect or party spirit. We needed no more organization or machinery than what was really necessary for the speedy evangelizing of the city. Surely we already had enough separate, rival church organizations on our hands, each working largely for its own interest, advancement, and glory.

The New Testament Church seemed to be drifting toward intellectualism. I became much burdened for it. During one meeting—it was so painful after what we had seen—I groaned aloud in prayer. One of the elders rebuked me severely for this. *"How are the mighty fallen"* (2 Samuel 1:19) kept ringing in my ears. A few of the most spiritual had the same burden with me. After this incident, prayer again seemed to prevail in a measure. We had a great meeting in the church one Sunday night, and one hundred knelt at the altar.

I met with the Peniel boys in Pasadena for prayer, and we had a breaking through time. We felt the Lord would soon work mightily. At Brother Brownley's tent at Seventh and Spring Streets, Los Angeles, we had a deep spirit of prayer and powerful altar services. There was a feeling that God was about to do something extraordinary. The spirit of prayer came more and more heavily upon us.

In Pasadena, before moving to Los Angeles, I would lie on my bed in the daytime and roll and groan under the burden. At night I could scarcely sleep for the spirit of prayer. I fasted much, not caring for food while burdened. At one time I was in soul travail for nearly twenty-four hours without intermission. It nearly used me up. Prayer literally consumed me. Sometimes I would groan all night in my sleep.

Prayer was not formal in those days. It was God-breathed. It came upon us and overwhelmed us. We did not work it up. We were gripped with real travail of soul by the Spirit that could no more be shaken off than could the birth pangs of a woman in travail, without doing absolute violence to the Spirit of God. It was real intercession by the Holy Spirit.

For several days I had an impression another letter was coming from Evan Roberts. It soon came and read as follows:

Loughor, Wales, November 14, 1905
My dear comrade: What can I say that will encourage you in this terrible fight? I find it is a most awful one. Praise God, the kingdom of the Evil One is being besieged on every side. Oh, the millions of prayers—not simply the form of prayer—but the soul finding its way right to the White Throne! People in Wales have prayed during the last year. May the Lord bless you with a mighty downpouring. In Wales it seems as if the Holy One rests upon the congregation, awaiting the opening of the hearts of the followers of Christ. We had a mighty downpouring of the Holy Spirit last Saturday night. This was preceded by the correcting of the people's views of true worship. 1. To give unto God, not to receive. 2. To please God, not to please ourselves. Therefore, looking to God and forgetting the Enemy, and also the fear of men, we prayed and the Spirit descended. I pray God to hear your prayer, to keep your faith strong, and to save California. I remain, your brother in the fight.
—Evan Roberts

This was the third letter I had received from Wales, from Evan Roberts, and I feel their prayers had much to do with our final victory in California.

Evan Roberts tells us of his own experience with God:

One Friday night last spring, while praying by my bedside before retiring, I was taken up to a great expanse, without time or space. It was communion with God. Before this I had had a far-off God. I was frightened that night, but never since. So great was my shivering that I rocked the bed, and my brother, being awakened, took hold of me, thinking I was ill.

Evan Roberts experienced this every night for three months, from 1 A.M. until 5 A.M. He wrote a message to the world about this time, as follows:

> The revival in South Wales is not of men, but of God. He has come very close to us. There is no question of creed or of dogma in this movement. We are teaching no sectarian doctrine, only the wonder and beauty of Christ's love. I have been asked concerning my methods. I have none. I never prepare what I shall speak, but leave that to Him. I am not the source of this revival, but only one agent among what is growing to be a multitude. I wish no personal following, but only the world for Christ.
>
> I believe that the world is upon the threshold of a great religious revival, and I pray daily that I may be allowed to help bring this about. Wonderful things have happened in Wales in a few weeks, but these are only a beginning. The world will be swept by His Spirit as by a rushing, mighty wind. Many who are now silent Christians will lead the movement. They will see a great light and will reflect this light to thousands now in darkness. Thousands will do more than we have accomplished, as God gives them power.

What beautiful humility! This is the secret of all power. An English eyewitness of the revival in Wales wrote,

Such real travail of soul for the unsaved I have never before witnessed. I have seen young Evan Roberts convulsed with grief and calling on his audience to pray. "Don't sing," he would exclaim; "it's too terrible to sing."

Conviction has often been lifted from the people by too much singing.

Another writer declared,

It was not the eloquence of Evan Roberts that broke men down, but his tears. He would break down, crying bitterly for God to bend them, in an agony of prayer, the tears coursing down his cheeks, his whole frame writhing. Strong men would break down and cry like children. Women would shriek. A sound of weeping and wailing would fill the air. Evan Roberts, in the intensity of his agony, would fall in the pulpit, while many in the crowd often fainted.

Of the later work in India we read,

The girls in India were wonderfully wrought upon and baptized with the Spirit (in Ramabai Mission), under conviction of their need. Great light was given to them. When delivered, they jumped up and down for joy for hours without fatigue; in fact, they were stronger for it. They cried out with the burning that came into and upon them. Some fell as they saw a great light pass before them, while the fire of God burned the members of the body of sin—pride, anger, love of the world, selfishness, uncleanness, and so on. They neither ate nor slept until the victory was won. Then the joy was so great that for two or three days after receiving the baptism of the Holy Spirit they did not care for food.

About twenty girls went into a trance at one time and became unconscious of this world for hours; some for three or four days. During that time they sang, prayed, clapped their hands, rolled about, or sat still. When they became conscious, they told of seeing a throne in heaven, a white-robed throng, and a glory so bright they could not bear it. Soon the whole place was aflame. School had to be suspended, they forgot to eat or sleep, and whole nights and days were absorbed in prayer. The Spirit was poured out upon one of the seeking girls in the night. Her companion sleeping next to her awoke, and seeing fire envelop her, ran across the dormitory and brought a pail of water to dash upon her. In less than an hour, nearly all the girls in the compound were weeping, praying, and confessing their sins. Many of these girls were invested with a strange, beautiful, and supernatural fire.

The spontaneous composition of hymns was a curious feature of some of the meetings in other parts of India. At Kara Camp, pictures appeared on the walls to a company of small girls in prayer, supernaturally depicting the life of Christ. The figures moved in the pictures and were in color. Each view would last from two to ten minutes, and then the light would gradually fade away, to reappear in a few moments with a new scene. These appeared for twelve hours and were seen not only by the native children of the orphanage and eight missionaries, but also by native Christians living nearby. Even heathens came to see the wonderful sight. These pictures were all faithfully depicting the Bible narration and were entirely supernatural. They had a tremendous effect in breaking up the hard hearts of the heathen. In Wales, colored lights were often seen, like balls of fire, during the revival there.

I kept going day and night to different missions, exhorting believers continually to prayer and faith for the revival. One night at the New Testament Church, during a deep spirit of prayer on the congregation, the Lord came suddenly so near that we could feel His presence as though He were closing in on us around the edges of the meeting. Two-thirds of the people sprang to their feet in alarm, and some ran hurriedly out of the meeting, even leaving their hats behind them, almost scared out of their senses. There was no out-of-the-ordinary demonstration in the natural to cause this fright. It was a supernatural manifestation of His nearness. What would such do if they saw the Lord?

I started a little cottage prayer meeting where we could have more liberty to pray and wait on the Lord. The spirit of prayer was being hindered, at times, in the other meetings. The more spiritual were hungry for this opportunity. However, the leaders misunderstood and opposed me. Then our landlady got the Devil in her and wanted to throw us out of our home. She was not right with God. Our rent was paid up, but the Enemy tried to use her. The fight was on. They began to oppose my ministry at the New Testament Church. A sister tried to persuade me to discontinue the prayer meetings I had started. I asked the Lord to show me His will in the matter. He came and filled our little cottage with a cloud of glory until I could scarcely bear His presence. That settled it for me. *"We ought to obey God rather than men"* (Acts 5:29). I suffered much criticism. I think they were afraid I would start another church. But I had no such thought at that time. I only wanted to have freedom to pray. Many a mission and church have gone on the rocks opposing God.

I wrote more articles for the religious press, of which the following are extracts:

> Slowly but surely, the conviction is coming upon the saints of southern California that God is going to pour out His Spirit here as in Wales. We are having faith for things such as we have never dreamed of, for the near future. We are assured of no less than a Pentecost for this whole country. But we can never have Pentecostal results without Pentecostal power. And this will mean Pentecostal demonstration. Few care to meet God face to face. Flesh and blood cannot inherit the kingdom of God.
>
> —*Christian Harvester*

> The current of revival is sweeping by our door. Will we cast ourselves on its mighty bosom and ride to glorious victory? A year of life at this time, with its wonderful possibilities for God, is worth a hundred years of ordinary life. Pentecost is knocking at our doors. The revival for our country is no longer a question. Slowly but surely, the tide has been rising until, in the very near future, we believe for a deluge of salvation that will sweep all before it. Wales will not long stand alone in this

glorious triumph for our Christ. The spirit of revival is coming upon us, driven by the breath of God, the Holy Spirit. The clouds are gathering rapidly, big with a mighty rain, whose precipitation lingers but a little.

Heroes will arise from the dust of obscure and despised circumstances, whose names will be emblazoned on heaven's eternal page of fame. The Spirit is brooding over our land again as at Creation's dawn, and the decree of God goes forth: *"Let there be light!"* (Genesis 1:3). Brother, sister, if we all believed God, can you realize what would happen? Many of us here are living for nothing else. A volume of believing prayer is ascending to the throne night and day. Los Angeles, southern California, and the whole continent shall surely find itself before long in the throes of a mighty revival, by the Spirit and power of God.

—*Way of Faith,* November 16, 1905

We had been for some time led to pray for a Pentecost. It seemed almost beginning. Of course we did not realize what a real Pentecost was. But the Spirit did, and led us to ask correctly. One afternoon, after a service in the New Testament Church, seven of us seemed providentially led to join hands and agree in prayer to ask the Lord to pour out His Spirit speedily, with *"signs following"* (Mark 16:20). Where we got the idea from at that time I do not know. He must have suggested it to us Himself. We did not have "tongues" in mind. I think none of us had ever heard of such a thing. This was in February 1906.

While at a prayer meeting, on my knees, the Lord told me to get up and go to Brother Brownley's tent at

Seventh and Spring Streets. He gave me a message for them. I went, greatly burdened, and after speaking we had a real "breaking up time," weeping before the Lord. I then wrote a moving tract on "Soul Travail." The Lord was dealing with me much also about His atoning blood. I spent another entire night in prayer with Brother Boehmer, and the Lord gave me a blessed ministry at Pasadena in different meetings. At one meeting, I lay for two hours helpless under a burden for souls. The battle was getting more and more earnest.

On March 26, I went to a cottage meeting on Bonnie Brae Street. Both white and black believers were meeting there for prayer. I had attended another cottage meeting shortly before this, where I first met a Brother Seymour. He had just come from Texas. He was a black man, blind in one eye, very plain, spiritual, and humble. He attended the meetings at Bonnie Brae Street.

At that time the Lord gave me another tract, entitled "The Last Call." This was used mightily to awaken the people. It read,

> And now, once more, at the very end of the age, God calls. The last call, the midnight cry, is now upon us, sounding clearly in our ears. God will give this one more chance, the last. A final call, a worldwide revival. Then judgment upon the whole world. Some tremendous event is about to transpire.

Chapter 2

The Fire Falls at Azusa

I went to Burbank Hall, the New Testament Church, Sunday morning, April 15. A black sister was there and spoke in tongues. This created a great stir. The people gathered in little companies on the sidewalk after the service, inquiring what this might mean. It seemed like Pentecostal "signs." We then learned that the Spirit had fallen a few nights before, April 9, at the little cottage on Bonnie Brae Street. They had been tarrying very earnestly for some time for an outpouring. A handful of black and white believers had been waiting there daily, but for some reason I was not privileged to be present at that particular meeting. I went to the Bonnie Brae meeting in the afternoon, however, and found God working mightily. We had been praying for many months for victory. Jesus was now "showing Himself alive" (see Acts 1:3) again to many. The pioneers had broken through for the multitude to follow.

There was a general spirit of humility manifested in the meeting, They were taken up with God. Evidently the Lord had found the little company at last, outside as always, through whom He could have His way. God had not chosen an established mission where this could be done. They were in the hands of men; the Spirit could not work. Others far more pretentious had failed. That which man esteems had been passed by once more, and the Spirit was born again in a humble "stable" outside ecclesiastical establishments.

A body must be prepared, in repentance and humility, for every outpouring of the Spirit. The preaching of the Reformation was begun by Martin Luther in a dilapidated building in the midst of the public square in Wittenberg, Germany. D'Aubigne describes it as follows:

> In the middle of the square at Wittenberg stood an ancient wooden chapel, thirty feet long and twenty feet wide, whose walls, propped up on all sides, were falling into ruin. An old pulpit made of planks, and three feet high, received the preacher. It was in this wretched place that the preaching of the Reformation began. It was God's will that that which was to restore His glory should have the humblest surroundings. It was in this wretched enclosure that God willed, so to speak, that His well-beloved Son should be born a second time. Among those thousands of cathedrals and parish churches with which the world is filled, there was not one at that time that God chose for the glorious preaching of eternal life.

In the revival in Wales, the great expounders of England had to come and sit at the feet of crude, hardworking miners, and see the wonderful works of God. I wrote for the *Way of Faith* at this time,

> The real thing is appearing among us. The Almighty will again measure swords with Pharoah's magicians. But many will reject Him and blaspheme. Many will fail to recognize Him, even among His professed followers. We have been praying and believing for a Pentecost. Will we receive it when it comes?

The present worldwide Pentecostal manifestation did not break out in a moment, like a huge prairie fire, and set the world on fire. In fact, no work of God ever appears that way. There is a necessary time for preparation. The finished article is not realized at the beginning. Men may wonder where it came from, not being conscious of the preparation, but there is always such. Every movement of the Spirit of God must also run the gauntlet of the Devil's forces. The Dragon stands before the bearing mother, ready to swallow up her child (Revelation 12:4).

So it was with the present Pentecostal work in its beginning. The Enemy did much counterfeiting. God kept the young child well hid for a season from the Herods, until it could gain strength and discernment to resist them. The flame was guarded jealously by the hand of the Lord from the winds of criticism, jealousy, unbelief, and so on. It went through about the same experiences that all revivals have. Its foes were both inside and out. Both Luther and Wesley experienced the same difficulties in their time. *"We have this treasure in earthen vessels"* (2 Corinthians 4:7). Every natural birth is surrounded by circumstances not entirely pleasant. God's perfect work is brought about in human imperfection. We are creatures of the Fall. Then why expect a perfect manifestation in this case? We are coming back to God.

John Wesley wrote of his time,

> Almost as soon as I was gone, two or three began to take their imaginations for impressions from God. Meantime, a flood of reproach came upon me from almost every quarter. Be not alarmed that Satan sows tares among the wheat of Christ. It has ever been so, especially on any remarkable outpouring of the Spirit, and ever will be, until the Devil is chained for a thousand years. Till then he will always ape and endeavor to counteract the work of the Spirit of Christ.

D'Aubigne has said, "A religious movement almost always exceeds a just moderation. In order that human nature may make one step in advance, its pioneers must take many."

Another writer said,

> Remember with what accompaniments of extravagance and fanaticism the doctrine of justification by faith was brought back under Luther. The wonder was, not that Luther had the courage to face pope and cardinals, but that he had the courage to endure the contempt which his own doctrines brought upon him, as espoused and paraded by fanatical advocates. Recall, too, the scandal and offense that attended the revival of heart piety under Wesley. What we denounce as error may be the "refraction of some great truth below the horizon."

John Wesley himself once prayed, after the revival had about died out for the time, "Oh, Lord, send us the old revival, without the defects; but if this cannot be, send it with all its defects. We must have the revival!"

Adam Clark said,

> Nature, along with Satan, will always mingle themselves, as far as they can, in the genuine work of the Spirit in order to discredit and destroy it. In great revivals of religion, it is almost impossible to prevent wildfire from getting in among the true fire.

Dr. Seiss said,

> Never, indeed, has there been a sowing of God on earth but it has been oversown by Satan; or a growth for Christ, which the plantings of the Wicked One did not mingle with and hinder. He who sets out to find a perfect church, in which there are no unworthy elements and no disfigurations, proposes to himself a hopeless task.

Still another writer wrote,

> In the various crises that have occurred in the history of the church, men have come to the front who have manifested a holy recklessness that astonished their fellows. When Luther nailed his theses to the door of the cathedral at Wittenberg, cautious men were astonished at his audacity. When John Wesley ignored all church restrictions and religious propriety and preached in the fields and byways, men declared his reputation was ruined. So it has been in all ages. When the religious condition of the times called for men who were willing to sacrifice all for

Christ, the demand created the supply, and there have always been found a few who were willing to be regarded reckless for the Lord. An utter recklessness concerning men's opinions and other consequences is the only attitude that can meet the needs of the present times.

God found His Moses, in the person of Brother Smale, to lead us to the Jordan crossing. But He chose Brother Seymour for our Joshua, to lead us over.

Sunday, April 15, the Lord called me to ten days of special prayer. I felt greatly burdened but had no idea of what He had particularly in mind. He had a work for me and wanted to prepare me for it. Wednesday, April 18, the terrible San Francisco earthquake came, which also devastated the surrounding cities and country. No less than five hundred lost their lives in San Francisco alone. I felt a deep conviction that the Lord was answering our prayers for a revival in His own way. *"When thy judgments are in the earth, the inhabitants of the world will learn righteousness"* (Isaiah 26:9). A tremendous burden of prayer came upon me that the people might not be indifferent to His voice.

Thursday, April 19, while sitting in the noon meeting at Peniel Hall, 227 South Main Street, the floor suddenly began to move with us. An unusual tremor ran through the room as Los Angeles was hit with a small earthquake. We sat in awe. Many people ran into the middle of the street, looking up anxiously at the buildings, fearing they were about to fall. It was an earnest time.

I went home and, after a season of prayer, was impressed by the Lord to go to the meeting that had been moved from Bonnie Brae Street to 312 Azusa Street. Here they had rented an old frame building, formerly a Methodist church, in the center of the city but now a long time out of use for meetings. It had become a receptacle for old lumber, plaster, and other materials. They had cleared space enough in the surrounding dirt and debris to lay some planks on top of empty nail kegs, with seats enough for possibly thirty people, if I remember rightly. These were arranged in a square, facing one another.

I was under tremendous pressure to get to the meeting that evening. It was my first visit to Azusa Mission. Mother Wheaton, who was living with us, was going with me. She was so slow that I could hardly wait for her. We finally reached Azusa and found about a dozen saints there, some white, some black. Brother Seymour was there, in charge. The "Ark of God" moved off slowly, but surely, at Azusa. It was carried on the shoulders of His own appointed priests in the beginning. We had no "new cart" in those days to please the carnal, *"mixed multitude"* (Exodus 12:38). We had the Devil to fight, but the Ark was not drawn by oxen (dumb beasts). The priests were *"alive unto God"* (Romans 6:11) through much preparation and prayer.

Discernment was not perfect, and the Enemy got some advantage that brought reproach to the work, but the saints soon learned to *"take forth the precious from the vile"* (Jeremiah 15:19). The combined forces of hell were set determinedly against us in the beginning. It was not all blessing. In fact, the fight was terrific. As always, the Devil combed the country for crooked spirits to destroy the work if possible. But the fire could not be smothered. Gradually the tide arose in victory. From a small beginning, a very little flame was kindled.

I gave a message at my first meeting at Azusa. Two of the saints spoke in tongues. Much blessing seemed to attend the utterance. It was soon noised abroad that God was working at Azusa, and all kinds of people began to come to the meetings. Many were curious and unbelieving, but others were hungry for God. The newspapers began to ridicule and abuse the meetings, thus giving us much free advertising. This brought the crowds. The Devil overdid himself again. Outside persecution never hurt the work. We had the most to fear from the working of evil spirits within. Even spiritualists and hypnotists came to investigate and to try their influence. Then all the religious sore-heads, crooks, and cranks came, seeking a place in the work. We had the most to fear from these. But this is always the danger to every new work; they had no place elsewhere. This condition cast a fear over many that was hard to overcome. It hindered the Spirit much. Many were afraid to seek God for fear the Devil might get them.

We found early in the Azusa work that when we attempted to steady the ark, the Lord stopped working. We dared not call the attention of the people too much to the working of the Evil One. Fear would follow. We could only pray—then God gave victory. There was a presence of God with us that, through prayer, we could depend on. The leaders had limited experience, and the wonder is that the work survived at all against its powerful adversaries. But it was of God. That was the secret.

A certain writer has well said,

> On the Day of Pentecost, Christianity faced the world, a new religion without a college, a people, or a patron. All that was ancient and venerable rose up before her in solid opposition, and she did not flatter or conciliate any one of them. She assailed every existing system and every bad habit, burning her way through innumerable forms of opposition. This she accomplished with her "tongue of fire" alone.

Another writer has said,

> The apostasy of the early church came as a result of a greater desire to see the spread of its power and rule than to see new natures given to its individual members. The moment we covet a large following and rejoice in the crowd that is attracted by our presentation of what we consider truth, and have not a greater desire to see the natures of individuals changed according to the divine plan, we start to travel the same road of apostasy that leads to Rome and her daughters.

I found the earthquake had opened many hearts. I was especially distributing my last tract, "The Last Call." It seemed very appropriate after the earthquake. Sunday, April 22, I took ten thousand of these to the New Testament Church. The workers seized them eagerly and scattered them quickly throughout the city.

Nearly every pulpit in the land was working overtime to prove that God had nothing to do with earthquakes and thus allay the fears of the people. The Spirit was striving to knock at hearts with conviction through this judgment. I felt indignation that the preachers should be used by Satan to drown out His voice. Even the teachers in the schools labored hard to convince the children that God was not in earthquakes. The Devil put on a big propaganda on this line.

I had been much in prayer since the earthquake and had slept little. After the earthquake in Los Angeles, the Lord told me that He definitely had a message to give me for the people. On the Saturday after, He gave me a part of it. On Monday the rest was given. I finished writing it at 12:30 A.M. on Tuesday, and it was ready for the printer. I kneeled before the Lord, and He met me in a powerful way, a powerful witness that the message was from Him. I was to have it printed in the morning. From that time until 4 A.M., I was wonderfully taken up in the spirit of intercession. I seemed to feel the wrath of God against the people and to withstand it in prayer. He showed me He was terribly grieved at their obstinacy in the face of His judgment on sin. San Francisco was a terribly wicked city.

He showed me all hell was being moved to drown out His voice in the earthquake. The message He had given me was to counteract this influence. Men had been denying His presence in the earthquake. Now He would speak. It was a terrific message He had given me. I was to argue the question with no man, but simply give them the message. They would answer to Him. I felt all hell against me in this, and so it proved. I went to bed at 4 o'clock, arose at 7, and hurried with the message to the printer.

The question in almost every heart was, "Did God do that?" But instinct taught men on the spot that He had. Even the wicked were conscious of the fact. The tract was set up quickly. The same day it was on the press, and the next noon I had my first consignment of the tract. I felt that I must hasten and get them to the people as quickly as possible. I was reminded that the ten days I was called by the Lord to prayer was up the very day I received the first of the tracts. I understood it all now.

I distributed the message speedily in the missions, churches, saloons, business houses, and, in fact, everywhere, both in Los Angeles and Pasadena. Besides, I mailed thousands to workers in nearby towns for distribution. The whole undertaking was a work of faith. I began without a dollar, but God supplied the money as needed. I worked hard every day. Brother and Sister Otterman distributed them in San Diego. It required courage. Many raved at the message. I went with them through all the dives in Los Angeles. All hell was stirred.

God sent Brother Boehmer from Pasadena to help me. Brother Boehmer stood outside and prayed while I went into the saloons with them. They were mad enough to kill me in some instances. Business was at a standstill after the news came from San Francisco. The people were paralyzed with fear. This accounted to some extent for the influence of my tract. The pressure against me was terrific. All hell was surging around me to stop the message. But I never faltered. I felt God's hand upon me continually in the matter. The people were appalled to see what God had to say about earthquakes. He sent me to a number of meetings with a solemn exhortation to repent and seek Him. At Azusa Mission we had a powerful time. The saints humbled themselves. A black sister both spoke and sang in tongues. The very atmosphere of heaven was there.

Sunday, May 11, I had finished my "Earthquake" tract distribution. Then the burden suddenly left me. My work was done. Seventy-five thousand had been published and distributed in Los Angeles and southern California in less than three weeks' time. In Oakland, Brother Manley, of his own volition, had printed and distributed fifty thousand more in the Bay Cities in about the same space of time.

The San Francisco earthquake was surely the voice of God to the people on the Pacific coast. It was used mightily in conviction for the revival the Lord graciously brought afterward. In the early Azusa days, both heaven and hell seemed to have come to town. Men were at the breaking point. Conviction was mightily on the people. They would fly to pieces even on the street, almost without provocation. A very "blood line" seemed to be drawn around Azusa Mission by the Spirit. When men came within two or three blocks of the place, they were seized with conviction.

The work was getting clearer and stronger at Azusa. God was working mightily. It seemed that everyone had to go to Azusa. Missionaries were gathered there from Africa, India, and the islands of the sea. Preachers and workers had crossed the continent and come from distant lands with an irresistible drawing to Los Angeles. *"Gather my saints together"* (Psalm 50:5). They had come up for "Pentecost," though they little realized it. It was God's call. Holiness meetings, tents, and missions began to close up for lack of attendance. Their people were at Azusa. Brother and Sister Garr closed the Burning Bush Hall, came to Azusa, received the baptism in the Spirit, and were soon on their way to India to spread the fire. Even Brother

Smale had to come to Azusa to look up his members. He invited them back home, promised them liberty in the Spirit, and for a time God worked mightily at the New Testament Church, also.

There was much persecution, especially from the press. They wrote us up shamefully, but this only drew the crowds. Some gave the work six months to live. Soon the meetings were running day and night. The place was packed out nightly. The whole building, up-stairs and down, had now been cleared and put into use. There were far more white people than black people coming. The "color line" was washed away in the blood of Christ. A. S. Worrell, a translator of the New Testament, declared the Azusa work had rediscovered the blood of Christ to the church at that time. Great emphasis was placed on Christ's blood, for cleansing and more. A high standard was held up for a clean life. *"When the enemy shall come in like a flood, the Spirit of the LORD shall lift up a standard against him"* (Isaiah 59:19).

Divine love was wonderfully manifest in the meetings. The people would not even allow an unkind word said against their opposers or the churches. The message was the love of God. It was a sort of *"first love"* (Revelation 2:4) of the early church returned. The baptism of the Holy Spirit, as we received it in the beginning, did not allow us to think, speak, or hear evil of any man. The Spirit was very sensitive, tender as a dove. The Holy Spirit is symbolized as a dove. We knew the moment we had grieved the Spirit by an un-kind thought or word. We seemed to live in a sea of pure divine love. The Lord fought our battles for us in those days. We committed ourselves to His judgment fully in all matters, never seeking to even defend the work or ourselves. We lived in His wonderful, immediate presence. And nothing contrary to His pure Spirit was allowed there.

The false was sifted out from the real by the Spirit of God. The Word of God itself decided absolutely all issues. The hearts of the people, both in act and motive, were searched to the very bottom. It was no joke to become one of that company. No man *"durst...join himself to them"* (Acts 5:13) unless he meant business. It meant a dying out and cleaning up process in those days to receive the baptism. We had a "tarrying room" upstairs for those especially seeking God for the Holy Spirit baptism, though many got it in the main assembly room also. In fact, they often got it in their seats in those days.

The Spirit worked very deeply in the tarrying room. An unquiet spirit or a thoughtless talker was immediately reproved by the Spirit. We were on holy ground (Exodus 3:5). This atmosphere was unbearable to those with a carnal spirit. They generally gave this room a wide berth unless they had been thoroughly subdued and burned out. Only honest seekers sought it, those who really meant business with God. It was no place to throw fits or blow off steam. Men did not "fly to their lungs" in those days. They flew to the mercy seat. They took their shoes off, figuratively speaking. They were on holy ground.

Arthur Booth-Clibborn has written the following weighty words:

> Any cheapening of the price of Pentecost would be a disaster of untold magnitude. The company in the Upper Room, upon whom

Pentecost fell, had paid the highest price for it. In this they approached as near as possible to Him who had paid the supreme price in order to send it. Do we ever really adequately realize how utterly lost to this world, how completely despised, rejected, and outcast was that company? Their Master and Leader had just passed through the "hangman's rope," so to speak, at the hands of the highest civilization of the day. Their Calvary was complete, and so a complete Pentecost came to match it. The latter will resemble the former in completeness. We may, therefore, each of us say to ourselves, "As your cross, so will your Pentecost be." God's way to Pentecost was via Calvary. Individually it must be so today also. The purity and fullness of the individual Pentecost must depend upon the completeness of the individual Calvary. This is an unalterable principle.

Friday, June 15, at Azusa, the Spirit dropped the "heavenly chorus" into my soul. I found myself suddenly joining the rest who had received this supernatural gift. It was a spontaneous manifestation and rapture no earthly tongue can describe. In the beginning, this manifestation was wonderfully pure and powerful. We feared to try to reproduce it, as with the tongues also. Now many seemingly have no hesitation in imitating all the gifts, causing them to lose their power and influence. No one could understand this gift of song but those who had it. It was indeed a *"new song"* in the Spirit (Psalm 40:3, for example). When I first heard it in the meetings, a great hunger entered my soul to receive it. I felt it would exactly express my pent-up feelings.

I had not yet spoken in tongues, but the "new song" captured me. It was a gift from God of high order. No one had preached it. The Lord had sovereignly bestowed it, with the outpouring of the "residue of oil," the *latter rain* baptism of the Spirit (James 5:7). It was exercised as the Spirit moved the possessors, either in solo fashion or by the company. It was sometimes without words, other times in tongues. The effect was wonderful on the people. It brought a heavenly atmosphere, as though the angels themselves were present and joining with us. And possibly they were. It seemed to still criticism and opposition and was hard for even wicked men to gainsay or ridicule.

Some have condemned this "new song" without words. But was not sound given before language? And is there not intelligence without language also? Who composed the first song? Must we necessarily always follow some man's composition before us? We are too much worshippers of tradition. The speaking in tongues is not according to man's wisdom or understanding; then why not a "gift of song"? It is certainly a rebuke to the "jazzy" religious songs of our day. And possibly it was given for that purpose. Yet some of the old hymns are very good to sing also. We need not despise them or treat them lightly. Someone has said that every fresh revival brings in its own hymnology. And this one surely did.

In the beginning in Azusa, we had no musical instruments. In fact, we felt no need for them. There was no place for them in our worship—all was spontaneous. We did not even sing from hymnals. All the old, well-known hymns were sung from memory, quickened by the Spirit of God. "The Comforter Has Come" was possibly the one most sung. We sang it from a fresh, powerful heart experience. Oh, how the power of God filled and thrilled us. Then the songs of Christ's blood were very popular. "The life is in the blood." Sinai, Calvary, and Pentecost all had their rightful place in the Azusa work. But the "new song" was altogether different, not of human composition. It cannot be successfully counterfeited. The crow cannot imitate the dove. But they finally began to despise this gift, when the human spirit asserted itself again. They drove it out by hymnals and selected songs by readers. It was like murdering the Spirit, and was most painful to some of us, but the tide was too strong against us.

Hymnals today are too largely a commercial proposition, and we would not lose much without most of them. Even the old tunes are often violated by change, and new styles must be gotten out every season for added profit. There is very little real spirit of worship in them. They move the toes, but not the hearts of men. The spirit of song given from God in the beginning was like the Aeolian harp in its spontaneity and sweetness. In fact, it was the very breath of God, playing on human heart strings, or human vocal cords. The notes were wonderful in sweetness, volume, and duration. In fact, they were often humanly impossible. It was indeed "singing in the Spirit."

Brother Seymour was recognized as the nominal leader in charge. But we had no pope or hierarchy. We were brethren. We had no human program; the Lord Himself was leading. We had no priest class, nor priest craft. These things have come in later, with the apostasizing of the movement. We did not even have a platform or pulpit in the beginning. All were on one level. The ministers were servants, according to the true meaning of the word. We did not honor men for their advantage in means or education, but rather for their God-given gifts. God set the members in the body. Now *"a wonderful and horrible thing is committed in the land. The prophets prophesy falsely, and the priests bear rule by their means; and my people love to have it so: and what will ye do in the end thereof"* (Jeremiah 5:30–31). Also, *"As for my people, children are their oppressors* [sometimes grown-up ones], *and women rule over them"* (Isaiah 3:12).

Brother Seymour generally sat behind two empty boxes, one on top of the other. He usually kept his head inside the top one during the meeting, in prayer. There was no pride there. The services ran almost continuously. Seeking souls could be found under the power almost any hour of the day or night. The place was never closed or empty. The people came to meet God—He was always there. Hence a continuous meeting. The meeting did not depend on the human leader. God's presence became more and more wonderful. In that old building, with its low rafters and bare floors, God broke strong men and women to pieces, and put them together again for His glory. It was a tremendous overhauling process. Pride and self-assertion, self-importance, and self-esteem could not survive there. The religious ego preached its own funeral sermon quickly.

No subjects or sermons were announced ahead of time, and no special speakers for such an hour. No one knew what might be coming, what God would do. All was spontaneous, ordered by the Spirit. We wanted to hear from God, through whomever He might speak. We had no respect of persons. The rich and educated were the same as the poor and ignorant, although the former found it much harder to die to self. We only recognized God. All were equal. No flesh might glory in His presence (1 Corinthians 1:29). He could not use the self-opinionated. Those were Holy Spirit meetings, led by the Lord. It had to start in poor surroundings to keep out the selfish, human element. All came down in humility together at His feet. They all looked alike and had all things in common, in that sense at least. The rafters were low; the tall must come down. By the time they got to Azusa, they were humbled, ready for the blessing. The fodder was thus placed for the lambs, not for giraffes. All could reach it.

We were delivered right there from ecclesiastical hierarchism and abuse. We wanted God. When we first reached the meeting, we avoided human contact and greeting as much as possible. We wanted to meet God first. We got our heads under a bench in the corner in prayer, and met men only in the Spirit, knowing them *"after the flesh"* no more (2 Corinthians 5:16). The meetings started themselves, spontaneously, in testimony, praise, and worship. The testimonies were never hurried by a call for "popcorn." We had no pre-arranged program to be jammed through on time. Our time was the Lord's. We had real testimonies, from fresh heart-experiences. Otherwise, the shorter the testimonies, the better. A dozen might be on their feet at one time, trembling under the mighty power of God. We did not have to get our cue from some leader; yet we were free from lawlessness. We were shut up to God in prayer in the meetings, our minds on Him.

All obeyed God, in meekness and humility. In honor we "preferred one another." (See Romans 12:10.) The Lord was liable to burst through anyone.

We prayed for this continually. Someone would finally get up, anointed for the message. All seemed to recognize this and gave way. It might be a child, a woman, or a man. It might be from the back seat or from the front. It made no difference. We rejoiced that God was working. No one wished to show himself. We thought only of obeying God. In fact, there was an atmosphere of God there that forbade anyone but a fool from attempting to put himself forward without the real anointing—and such did not last long. The meetings were controlled by the Spirit, from the throne. Those were truly wonderful days. I often said that I would rather live six months at that time than fifty years of ordinary life. But God is just the same today. Only we have changed.

Someone might be speaking. Suddenly the Spirit would fall upon the congregation. God Himself would give the altar call. Men would fall all over the house, like the slain in battle, or rush for the altar en masse to seek God. The scene often resembled a forest of fallen trees. Such a scene cannot be imitated. I never saw an altar call given in those early days. God Himself would call them. And the preacher knew when to quit. When God spoke, we all obeyed. It seemed a fearful thing to hinder or grieve the Spirit. The whole place was steeped in prayer. God was in His holy temple. It was for man to keep silent. The Shekinah glory rested there. In fact, some claim to have seen the glory by night over the building. I do not doubt it. I have stopped more than once within two blocks of the place and prayed for strength before I dared go on. The presence of the Lord was so real.

Presumptuous men would sometimes come among us. Especially preachers who would try to spread their opinions. But their efforts were short-lived. The breath would be taken from them. Their minds would wander, their brains reel. Things would turn black before their eyes. They could not go on. I never saw one get by with it in those days. They were up against God. No one cut them off; we simply prayed—the Holy Spirit did the rest. We wanted the Spirit to control. He wound them up in short order. They were carried out dead, spiritually speaking. They generally bit the dust in humility, going through the process we had all gone through. In other words, they died out, and came to see themselves in all their weakness. Then, in childlike humility and confession, they were taken up by God and transformed through the mighty baptism in the Spirit. The *"old man"* (Romans 6:6) died with all his pride, arrogance, and good works. In my own case, I came to abhor myself. I begged the Lord to drop a curtain so close behind me on my past that it would hit my heels. He told me to forget every good deed as though it had never occurred, as soon as it was accomplished, and go forward again as though I had never accomplished anything for Him, lest my good works become a snare to me.

We saw some wonderful things in those days. Even very good men came to abhor themselves in the clearer light of God. Often, it was hardest for preachers to die to self. They had so much to die to—so much reputation and good works. But when God got through with them, they gladly turned a new page and chapter. That was one reason they fought so hard. Death to self is not at all a pleasant experience. And strong men die hard.

Brother Ansel Post, a Baptist preacher, was sitting on a chair in the middle of the floor one evening in the meeting. Suddenly the Spirit fell upon him. He sprang from his chair, began to praise God in a loud voice in tongues, and ran all over the place, hugging all the brethren he could get hold of. He was filled with divine love. He later went to Egypt as a missionary. This is his own testimony:

> As suddenly as on the Day of Pentecost, while I was sitting some twelve feet right in front of the speaker, the Holy Spirit fell upon me and filled me literally. I seemed to be lifted up, for I was in the air in an instant, shouting, "Praise God," and instantly I began to speak in another language. I could not have been more surprised if at the same moment someone had handed me a million dollars.
>
> —Ansel Post, in *Way of Faith*

After Brother Smale had invited his people back and promised them liberty in the Spirit, I wrote the following in *Way of Faith:*

> The New Testament Church received her Pentecost yesterday. We had a wonderful time. Men and women were prostrate under the power all over the hall. A heavenly atmosphere pervaded the place. Such singing I have never heard before, the very melody of heaven. It seemed to come directly from the throne.
>
> —June 1906

In the *Christian Harvester* I wrote on the same date:

> At the New Testament Church, a young lady of refinement was prostrate on the floor for hours, while at times the most heavenly singing would issue from her lips. It would swell as

though reaching the throne and then die away in an almost unearthly melody. She sang, "Praise God! Praise God!" All over the house men and women were weeping. A preacher was flat on his face on the floor, dying to himself. Pentecost has fully come.

We had several all-night prayer meetings at the New Testament Church. But Pastor Smale never received the baptism of the Spirit with the speaking in tongues. He was in a trying position. It was all new to him, and the Devil did his worst to bring the work into disrepute and destroy it. He sent wicked spirits among us to frighten the pastor and cause him to reject it.

But Brother Smale was God's Moses, to lead the people as far as the Jordan, though he himself never got across. Brother Seymour led them over. And yet, strange to say, Seymour did not speak in tongues himself until some time after Azusa had been opened. Many of the saints entered in before him. All who received this baptism of the Spirit spoke in tongues.

Many stumbled in the beginning at Azusa because of the nature of the instruments first used. I wrote in *Way of Faith* as follows:

> Someone has said, it is not the man who can build the biggest brush heap, but rather the one who can set his heap on fire that will light up the country. God can never wait for a perfect instrument to appear. If so, He would certainly be waiting yet. Luther himself declared he was but a rough woodsman, to fell the trees. Pioneers are of that nature. God has more polished servants to follow up and trim and shape the timber symmetrically. A charge of dynamite

does not produce the finished product, but it does set loose the stones that later stand as monuments under the sculptor's skilled hand. Many high dignitaries of the Roman Church in Luther's time were convinced of the need for reformation, and they knew that he was on the right track. But they declared, in so many words, that they could never consent that this new doctrine should issue from "such a corner." That it should be a monk, a poor monk, who presumes to reform us all is what we cannot tolerate, they said. *"Can there any good thing come out of Nazareth?"* (John 1:46).

Fallen humanity is such a peculiar thing at its best, so shattered that it is very imperfect. *"We have this treasure in earthen vessels"* (2 Corinthians 4:7). In the embryonic stage of all new experiences, much allowance must be made for human frailty. There are always many coarse, impulsive, imperfectly balanced spirits among those first reached by a revival. Then, our understanding of the Spirit of God is so limited that we are always liable to make a mistake, failing to recognize all that may be really of God. We can understand fully only in the measure that we ourselves possess the Spirit. Snap judgment is always dangerous. *"Judge nothing before the time"* (1 Corinthians 4:5). The company used at Azusa Mission to break through were the "Gideon's band" that opened the way to victory for those to follow.

I wrote further in *Way of Faith*, August 1, 1906:

Pentecost has come to Los Angeles, the American Jerusalem. Every sect, creed, and doctrine under heaven is found in Los Angeles, as well as every nation represented. Many times

I have been tempted to wonder if my strength would hold out to see it. The burden of prayer has been very great. But since the spring of 1905, when I first received this vision and burden, I have never doubted the final outcome of it. Men are now troubled in soul everywhere, and the revival with its unusual phenomena is the topic of the day. There is terrible opposition manifested also. The newspapers here are very venomous and most unfair and untrue in their statements. The pseudo systems of religion are fighting hard also. But *"the hail shall sweep away the refuge of lies"* (Isaiah 28:17). Their "hiding places" are being uncovered. A cleansing stream is flowing through the city. The Word of God prevails.

Persecution is strong. Already the police have been asked to break up the meetings. The work has been hindered much also by fanatical spirits, of which the city has far too many. It is God and the Devil, a battle royal. We can do little but look on and pray. The Holy Spirit Himself is taking the lead, setting aside all human leadership largely. And woe to the man who gets in His way, selfishly seeking to dictate or control. The Spirit will not tolerate interference of this kind. The human instruments are largely lost sight of. Our hearts and minds are directed to the Lord. The meetings are crowded out. There is great excitement among the unspiritual and unsaved.

Every false religion under heaven is found represented here. Next to old Jerusalem there is nothing like it in the world. It is on the opposite side, nearly halfway around the world, with natural conditions very similar also. All nations are represented as at Jerusalem. Thousands are here from all over the Union and from many parts of the world, sent by God for "Pentecost." These will scatter the fire to the ends of the earth. Missionary zeal is at white heat. The gifts of the Spirit are being given, the church's armor restored. Surely we are in the days of restoration, the last days, wonderful and glorious days. But awful days for those who refuse God's call. They are days of privilege, responsibility, and peril.

Demons are being cast out, the sick healed, many blessedly saved, restored, and baptized with the Holy Spirit and power. Heroes are being developed, the weak made strong in the Lord. Men's hearts are being searched as with a lighted candle. It is a tremendous sifting time, not only of actions, but of inner secret motives. Nothing can escape the all-searching eye of God. Jesus is being lifted up, His blood magnified, and the Holy Spirit honored once more. There is much "slaying power" manifest—and this is the chief cause of resistance on the part of those who refuse to obey. It is real business. God is with us in great earnestness; we dare not trifle. Strong men lie for hours under the mighty power of God, cut down like grass. The revival will be a worldwide one, without doubt.

Some time later the pastor of the Trinity Church, Methodist Episcopal South, of Los Angeles, uttered the following words: "Here on the Pacific coast, where the sons of men meet from every quarter of the globe, prophetic souls believe the greatest moral and spiritual battles are to be fought—the Armageddon of the world."

Evan Roberts' "Message to the Churches" was voiced by him in the following lines of an old poem:

While the fire of God is falling,
While the voice of God is calling,
Brothers, get the flame.
While the torch of God is burning,
Men's weak efforts overturning,
Christians, get the flame.

While the Holy Ghost is pleading,
Human methods superseding,
He himself the flame.
While the power hard hearts are bending,
Yield thy own, to Him surrendering,
All to get the flame.

For the world at last is waking,
And beneath His spell is breaking,
Into living flame.
And our glorious Lord is seeking,
Human hearts, to rouse the sleeping,
Fired with heavenly flame.

If in utter self-surrender,
You would work with Christ, remember,
You must get the flame.
For the sake of bruised and dying,
And the lost in darkness lying,
We must get the flame.

For the sake of Christ in glory,
And the spreading of the story,
We must get the flame.
Oh, my soul, for thy refining,
And thy clearer, brighter shining,
Do not miss the flame.

> On the Holy Ghost relying,
> Simply trusting and not trying,
> You will get the flame.
> Brothers, let us cease our dreaming,
> And while God's floodtide is streaming,
> We will have the flame.

I wrote a little tract in June 1906, of which the following are extracts:

> Opportunity once passed is lost forever. There is a time when the tide is sweeping by our door. We may then plunge in and be carried to glorious blessing, success, and victory. To stand shivering on the bank, timid or paralyzed with stupor at such a time, is to miss all, and most miserably fail, both for time and for eternity. Oh, our responsibility! The mighty tide of God's grace and favor is even now sweeping by us in its prayer-directed course. *"There is a river* [of salvation], *the streams whereof shall make glad the city of God"* (Psalm 46:4). It is time to get together and plunge in, individually and collectively. We are baptized *"by one Spirit... into one body"* (1 Corinthians 12:13). Let us lay aside all carnal contentions and divisions that separate us from each other and from God. If we are of His body, we are *"one body."* The opportunity of a lifetime—of centuries—is at our door, to be eternally gained or lost. There is no time to hesitate. Act quickly, lest another *"take thy crown"* (Revelation 3:11). Oh, church of Christ, awake! Be baptized with power. Then fly to rescue others and to meet your Lord.

Gordon said, "If Antichrist is about to make his mightiest and most malignant demonstration, ought not the church to confront him with mighty displays of the Spirit's saving power?"

A. B. Simpson said,

> We are to witness, before the Lord's return, a real missionary "tongues" like those of Pentecost, through which the heathen world shall hear in their own language *"the wonderful works of God"* (Acts 2:11), and this perhaps on a scale whose vastness we have scarcely dreamed. Thousands of missionaries will go forth in one last mighty crusade from a united body of believers at home to bear swift witness of the crucified and coming Lord to all nations.

Arthur T. Pierson has said,

> The most alarming peril of today is naturalism—the denial of all direct divine agency and control. Science is uniting with unbelief, wickedness and worldliness, skepticism and materialism, to rule a personal God out of the universe. This drift toward materialism and naturalism demands the supernatural as its only corrective. In Enoch's time human sin was fast making atheists, and God *"took him"* (Genesis 5:24), spirit, soul, and body, so that men might be startled with the proof of a divine being and an invisible world. In Elijah's day, general apostasy was rebuked by the descent of horses and chariots of fire. And if ever men needed to be confronted with fruits of power above nature—a living God back of all the forces and machinery He controls, who does answer prayer, guide by His providences, and convert by His grace—it is now.

Oh, our weakness! Oh, our unbelief! May the Lord help us get back to Pentecostal experiences. *"When the Son of man cometh, shall he find faith on the earth?"* (Luke 18:8).

In Spurgeon's dying appeal, he said,

> The presence of God in the church will put an end to infidelity. Men will not doubt His Word when they feel His Spirit. For a thousand reasons, we need that Jehovah should come into the camp, as aforetimes He visited and delivered His people from bondage in Egypt.

Chapter 3

Deeper Yet

August 8, 1906, I rented a church building at the corner of Eighth and Maple Streets for a Pentecostal mission. I was led to this church in February while it was still occupied by the "Pillar of Fire" people. I had been impressed to pray for a building for services after I found the New Testament Church not going ahead, but I had not even known of the existence of this building. One day, unexpectedly, I was passing by and saw it for the first time. I noticed it had been a German church and was out of regular use. Through curiosity I opened the door, which was unlocked, and entered. I found the "Pillar of Fire" had it. Kneeling at the altar for a season of prayer, the Lord spoke to me, and I received a wonderful witness of the Spirit. In a moment I was walking the aisles claiming it for "Pentecost." Over the door was a large motto painted, "Gott ist die Liebe" (God Is Love). This was two months before the Azusa work began.

I looked no further for a building, knowing that God had spoken. One night, six months later, in August, I was passing that way and saw a sign, "For Rent," on the church. It had just been vacated. The Lord spoke to me: "There is your church."

"The Pillar of Fire" had gone up in smoke, not being able to raise the rent. They had been the most bitter opposers of the Azusa work. The Lord had vacated the building for us. The next day, I was led to tell our landlord, Brother Fred Shepard, of the situation. I did not ask him to help me, but the Lord had sent me to him. He asked how much the rent was, went into another room, and returned quickly with a check for fifty dollars. This was the first month's rent, and I secured the place at once.

The truth must be told. Azusa began to fail the Lord also early in her history. God showed me one day that they were going to organize, though not a word had been said in my hearing about it. The Spirit revealed it to me. He had me warn them against making a "party" spirit of the Pentecostal work. The Spirit-baptized saints were to remain one body, even as they had been called, and to be free as His Spirit was free, not *"entangled again with the yoke of* [ecclesiastical] *bondage"* (Galatians 5:1). The New Testament Church saints had already arrested their further progress in this way. God wanted a revival company, a channel through whom He could evangelize the world, blessing all people and believers. He could naturally not accomplish this with a sectarian party. That spirit has been the curse and death of every revival body sooner or later. History repeats itself in this matter.

Sure enough, the very next day after I had spoken this warning in the meeting, I found a sign outside the building reading "Apostolic Faith Mission." The Lord said, "That is what I told you." They had done it. Surely a party spirit cannot be Pentecostal. There can be no divisions in a true Pentecost. To formulate a separate body is but to advertise our failure as a people of God. It proves to the world that we cannot get along together, rather than causing them to believe in our salvation. *"That they may all be one;...that the world may believe"* (John 17:21).

From that time the trouble and division began. It was no longer a free Spirit for all as it had been. The work had become one more rival party and body, along with the other churches and sects of the city. No wonder the opposition steadily increased from the churches. We had been called to bless and serve the whole body of Christ everywhere. Christ is one, and His body can be but "one." To divide it is but to destroy it, just as with the natural body. *"By one Spirit are we all baptized into one body"* (1 Corinthians 12:13). The church is an organism, not a human organization.

They later tried to pull the work on the whole coast into this organization, but miserably failed. The work has spread as far as Portland and Seattle. God's people must be free from hierarchism. They are "blood-bought," and not their own. An earlier work in Texas later tried to gather in the Pentecostal missions on the Pacific coast and Los Angeles, but they also failed. Why should they claim authority over us? The revival in California was unique and separate as to origin. It came from heaven, even Brother Seymour not

71

receiving the baptism until many others had entered in here. He did not arrive in Los Angeles until the eleventh hour. The great battle from the beginning, both in Los Angeles and elsewhere, has been the conflict between the flesh and the Spirit, between Ishmael and Isaac.

At Eighth and Maple Streets, the Spirit was mightily manifest from the very first meeting. He was given complete control. The atmosphere was heavy with God's presence. One had to get right in order to remain at Eighth and Maple. *"Fearfulness...*[truly] *surprised the hypocrites"* (Isaiah 33:14). For some days we could do little but lie before the Lord in prayer.

The atmosphere was almost too sacred and holy to attempt to minister. Like the priests in the tabernacle of old, we could not minister because the glory was so great. In spite of this, however, we had terrible battles with fleshly professors and deceivers, and the Spirit was much grieved by contentious spirits. But God gave the victory. The atmosphere at Eighth and Maple was for a time even deeper than at Azusa. God came so wonderfully near us that the very atmosphere of heaven seemed to surround us. Such a divine *"weight of glory"* (2 Corinthians 4:17) was upon us that we could only lie on our faces. For a long time we could hardly even remain seated. All would be on their faces on the floor, sometimes during the whole service. I was seldom able to keep from lying full-length on the floor on my face. There was a little rise of about a foot, for a platform, when we moved into the church. On this I generally lay, while God ran the meetings. They were His meetings. Every night the power of God was mightily with us. It was glorious! The Lord seemed almost visible, He was so real.

We had the greatest trouble with strange preachers who wanted to preach. Of all people, they seemed to have the least sense and did not know enough to keep still before Him. They liked to hear themselves. But many a preacher died to self in these meetings. The city was full of them, just as today. They rattled like a last year's bean pod. We had a regular "dry bone" yard. (See Ezekiel 37:1–10.)

We always recognized Azusa as having been the mother mission, and there was never any friction or jealousy between us. We visited back and forth. Brother Seymour often met with us. I wrote in the *Christian Harvester* at that time, as follows:

> The meetings at Eighth and Maple are marvelous. We had the greatest time yesterday that I have ever seen. All day long the power of God swept the place. The church was crowded. Mighty conviction seized the people. The Spirit ran the meeting from start to finish. There was no program, and hardly a chance even for necessary announcements. No attempt was made to preach. A few messages were given by the Spirit. Everybody was free to obey God. The altar was full of seeking souls all day. A Free Methodist preacher's wife came through to a mighty baptism, speaking something like Chinese. All who received the baptism of the Spirit spoke in tongues. There were at least six Holiness preachers, some of them gray-headed, honored, and trusted for fruitful service for years, seeking the baptism most earnestly. They simply threw up their hands in the face of this revelation from God and stopped to tarry for their Pentecost. The president of the Holiness

Church of Southern California was one of the first at the altar, seeking earnestly.

Again I wrote in the same paper,

The Spirit allows little human interference in the meetings, generally passing mistakes by unnoticed, or moving them out of the way Himself. Things that ordinarily we would feel must be corrected are often passed over, and a worse calamity averted thereby. To draw attention to them brings the spirit of fear on the saints, and they stop seeking. The Spirit is hindered from working. He moves them out of the way. There are greater issues at stake at present. We try to keep them from magnifying Satan's power. We are preaching a big Christ instead. And God is using babes.

The Enemy is moving hell to break up our fellowship through doctrinal differences, but we must preserve the unity of the Spirit by all means. Some things can be adjusted later. They are much less important. God will never give this work into the hands of men. If it ever gets under man's control, it is done. Many would join themselves to us if they did not need to "lose their heads" and get small.

On the afternoon of August 16, at Eighth and Maple, the Spirit manifested Himself through me in tongues. There were seven of us present at the time. It was a weekday. After a time of testimony and praise, with everything quiet, I was softly walking the floor, praising God in my spirit. All at once I seemed to hear in my soul (not with my natural ears), a rich voice speaking in a language I did not know. I have later heard something similar to it in India. It seemed to envelop and fully satisfy the pent-up praises in my being. In a few moments I found myself, seemingly without volition on my part, enunciating the same sounds with my own vocal organs. It was an exact continuation of the same expression that I had heard in my soul a few moments before. It seemed a perfect language. I was almost like an outside listener. I was fully yielded to God and simply carried by His will, as on a divine stream. I could have hindered the expression but would not have done so for worlds. A heaven of conscious bliss accompanied it. It is impossible to describe the experience accurately. It must be experienced to be appreciated. There was no effort made to speak on my part and not the least possible struggle. The experience was most sacred, the Holy Spirit playing on my vocal chords, as on an Aeolian harp. The whole utterance was a complete surprise to me. I had never really been solicitous to speak in tongues. Because I could not understand it with my natural mind, I had rather feared it.

I had no desire at the time to even know what I was saying. It seemed a spiritual expression purely, outside the realm of the natural mind or understanding. I was truly "sealed in the forehead," ceasing from the works of my own natural mind fully. I wrote my experience for publication later in the following words:

> The Spirit had gradually prepared me for this culmination in my experience, both in prayer for myself and others. I had thus drawn nigh to God, my spirit greatly subdued. A place of utter abandonment of will had been reached, in absolute consciousness of helplessness, purified from natural self-activity. This process

had been cumulative. The presence of the Spirit within had been as sensitive to me as the water in the glass indicator of a steam boiler. My mind, the last fortress of man to yield, was taken possession of by the Spirit. The waters that had been gradually accumulating went over my head. I was possessed by Him fully. The utterance in tongues was without human mixture, *"as the Spirit gave...utterance"* (Acts 2:4).

Oh, the thrill of being fully yielded to Him! My mind had always been very active. Its natural workings had caused me most of my trouble in my Christian experience: *"Casting down reasonings"* (2 Corinthians 10:5, margin). Nothing hinders faith and the operation of the Spirit so much as the self-assertiveness of the human soul, the wisdom, strength, and self-sufficiency of the human mind. This must all be crucified, and here is where the fight comes in. We must become utterly undone, insufficient, and helpless in our own consciousness, thoroughly humbled, before we can receive full possession of the Holy Spirit. We want the Holy Spirit, but the fact is that He is wanting possession of us.

In my case, in the experience of speaking in tongues, I reached the climax in abandonment. This opened the channel for a new ministry of the Spirit in service. From that time, the Spirit began to flow through me in a new way. Messages would come, with anointings, in a way I had never known before. The spontaneous inspiration and illumination was truly wonderful, accompanied by convincing power. The full Pentecostal baptism spells complete abandonment, or possession by the Holy Spirit, of the whole man with a spirit of instant obedience. I had known much of the power of God for service for many years before this, but I now realized a sensitivity to the Spirit, a yieldedness, that made it possible for God to possess and work in new ways and channels, with far more powerful, direct results.

In the experience, I also received a new revelation of His sovereignty, both in purpose and action, such as I had never known before. I found I had often charged God with a seeming lack of interest or tardiness of action, when I should have yielded to Him, in faith, so that He might be able to work through me His sovereign will. I went into the dust of humility at this revelation of my own stupidity and His sovereign care and desire. I saw that the little bit of desire I possessed for His service was only the little bit that He had been able to get to me of His great desire and interest and purpose. His Word declares it. All there was of good in me, in thought or action, had come from Him. Like Hudson Taylor, I now felt that He was asking me simply to go with Him to help in that which He alone had purposed and desired. I felt very small in the light of this revelation and my past misunderstanding. He had existed, and had been working out His eternal purpose, long before I had ever been thought of—and will be long after I am gone.

There was no strain or contortions. No struggle in an effort to get the baptism. With me it was simply a matter of yielding. In fact, it was the opposite of struggle. There was no swelling of the throat, no "operation" to be performed on my vocal organs. I had not the slightest difficulty in speaking in tongues. And yet I can understand how some may have such difficulties. They are not fully yielded to God. With me the battle had been long drawn out. I had already worn myself out and fully yielded. God deals with no two individuals alike. I was not really seeking the baptism when I got it. And in fact, I never actually sought it as a definite experience. I wanted to be yielded fully to God, but beyond that I had no real definite expectation or desire. I wanted more of Him, that was all.

There was no shouting crowd around me to confuse or excite me. No one was suggesting tongues to me at the time, either by argument or imitation. Thank God He is able to do His work without such help, and often far better without it. I do not believe in dragging the child forth, spiritually speaking, with instruments. I do believe in sane, earnest prayer-help in the Spirit. Too many souls are dragged from the womb of conviction by force and have to be incubated ever after. As with nature, so in grace. It is best to dispense as far as possible with the doctors and old midwives. The child is almost killed at times through their unnatural violence. A pack of jackals over their prey could hardly act more fiercely than we have witnessed in some cases. In natural childbirth, it is generally best to let the mother alone as far as possible. We should teach and stand by to encourage, but not force the deliverance. Natural births are better.

I had been shut up largely to a ministry of intercession and prophecy before I reached this condition of utter abandonment to the Spirit. I was now to go forth again in service. When my day of Pentecost was fully come, the channel was cleared. The living waters burst forth. The door of my service sprang open at the touch of the hand of a sovereign God. The Spirit began to operate within me in a new and mightier way. It was a distinct, fresh climax and development, an epochal experience for me.

I now knew that I had tasted that for which we had been shut up as a company. In fact, this has proven an epoch in the history of the church just as distinct and definite as the Spirit's action in the time of Luther and Wesley, and with far greater portend. And it is not yet all history. We are too close to it yet to understand or appreciate it fully. But we have made another step back on the way to the restoration of the church as in the beginning. We are completing the circle. Jesus will return for a perfect church, "without spot or wrinkle." (See Ephesians 5:27.) He is coming for one body, not a dozen. He is the Head, and as such He is no monstrosity, with a hundred bodies. *That they all may be one;...that the world may believe"* (John 17:21). This, after all, is the greatest sign to the world. *"Though* [we] *speak with the tongues of men and of angels, and have not charity"* (1 Corinthians 13:1).

I felt after the experience of speaking in tongues that languages would come easy to me. And so it has proven. Also, I have learned to sing in the Spirit, although I never was a singer and do not know music.

I never sought tongues. My natural mind resisted the idea. This phenomenon necessarily violates human reason. It means abandonment of this faculty for the time. And this is "foolishness" and a stone of stumbling to the natural mind or reason. (See 1 Corinthians 2:14.) It is supernatural. We need not expect anyone who has not reached this depth of abandonment in his human spirit, this death to his own reason, to either accept or understand it. The natural reason must be yielded in the matter. There is a gulf to cross between reason and revelation, and it is this principle in experience that leads to the Pentecostal baptism. It is the underlying principle of this baptism. This is why the simple people usually get in first, though perhaps not always so well-balanced or capable otherwise. They are like the little boys going swimming—to use a homely illustration. They get in first because they have the least clothes to divest themselves of. We must all come "naked" into this experience.

The early church lived in this as its normal atmosphere. Hence its abandonment to the working of the Spirit, its supernatural gifts, and its power. Our "wiseacres" (those who pretend to know the power of the Spirit) cannot reach this. Oh, to become a fool, to know nothing in ourselves, so that we might receive the mind of Christ.

I do not mean to say that we must talk in tongues continually. The baptism is not all tongues. We can live in this place of illumination and abandonment and still speak in our own language. The Bible was not written in tongues. We may surely live in the Spirit at all times. Oh, the depth of abandonment—all self gone—conscious of knowing nothing, of having nothing, except as the Spirit will teach and impart to us. This is the true place of power in the ministry of service. There is nothing left but God, the pure Spirit. Every hope or sense of capability in the natural is gone.

We live by His breath, as it were. The *"wind"* on the Day of Pentecost was the breath of God (Acts 2:2). But what more can we say? It must be experienced to be understood. It cannot be explained. We have certainly had a measure of the Spirit before without this. To this fact all history testifies, but we cannot have the Pentecostal baptism without it. The apostles received it suddenly and in full. Only simple faith and abandonment can receive, for human reason can find all kinds of flaws and apparent foolishness in it.

I spoke in tongues possibly for about fifteen minutes on this first occasion. Then the immediate inspiration passed away, for the time. I have spoken at times since also, but I never try to reproduce it. It would be foolishness and sacrilege to try to imitate it. The experience left behind it the consciousness of a state of utter abandonment to the Lord, a place of perfect rest from my own works and activity of mind. It left with me a consciousness of utter God-control, and of His presence naturally in corresponding measure. It was a most sacred experience.

Many have trifled foolishly with this principle and possession. They have failed to continue in the Spirit and have caused others to stumble. This has brought about great harm. But the experience still remains as a fact, both in history and in present-day realization. The greater part of most Christians' knowledge of God is and has always been, since the loss of the Spirit by the early church, an intellectual knowledge. Their knowledge of the Word and principles of God is an intellectual one, through natural reasoning and understanding largely. They have little revelation, illumination, or inspiration directly from the Spirit of God.

The famous commentators, Conybeare and Howson, write,

> This gift [speaking in tongues] was the result of a sudden influx of the supernatural to

the believer. Under its influence, the exercise of the understanding was suspended while the spirit was wrapped in a state of sheer joy by the immediate communication of the Spirit of God. In this joyful state, the believer was constrained by irresistible power to pour forth his feelings of thanksgiving and rapture in words not his own. He was usually even ignorant of their meaning.

Stalker, in his *Life of Paul,* has the following to say:

It [the speaking in tongues] seems to have been a kind of utterance in which the speaker poured out an impassioned rhapsody, by which his religious faith received both expression and exaltation. Some were not able to tell others the meaning of what they were saying, while others had this additional power; and there were those who, though not speaking in tongues themselves, were able to interpret what the inspired speakers were saying. In all cases, there seems to have been a kind of immediate inspiration, so that what they did was not the effect of calculation or preparation, but of a strong, present impulse.

These phenomena are so remarkable that, if narrated in a history, they would put a severe strain on Christian faith. They show with what mighty force, at its first entrance into the world, Christianity took possession of the spirits it touched.

The very gifts of the Spirit were perverted into instruments of sin; for those possessed of the more showy gifts, such as miracles and tongues, were too fond of displaying them, and turned them into grounds of boasting.

There is always danger attached to privileges. Children frequently cut themselves with sharp knives. However, we are certainly in more danger from remaining in stagnation, where we are, than in going ahead trustingly for God.

Describing some of my personal experiences, prior to experiencing this baptism, I wrote the following in *Christian Harvester:*

> My own heart was searched until I cried out under the added light, "God, deliver me from my religious self-consciousness!" Seldom have I suffered in humility, shame, and reproach, as at this vision of my very best in the sight of God. My religious comeliness was indeed turned into corruption. I felt that I could not bear to hear or even to think of it again. I felt I would be glad to forget even my own name and identity. So with extreme satisfaction, I destroyed records of my past achievements for God, upon which my eyes had loved to linger. I now abhorred them, as a temptation from the Devil to self-exaltation. Letters of commendation for religious services rendered, literary works of seeming excellence to me, and sermons that to me had seemed wonderful in knowledge and construction, now actually nauseated me, because of the element of self-pride detected in them. I found I had come to rest on these for expected divine favor and reward. "Nothing but the blood of Jesus" had at least partially been lost sight of. I was depending also on these other things to recommend me to God. In this lay great danger; so I destroyed

these treasured documents, false evidences, as I would a viper, lest they tempt me from the sufficiency of His merits alone. It meant a deep heart searching.

Past services now became a complete blank to me, and with the greatest relief on my part. I began again for God as though I had never accomplished anything. I felt that I stood before Him empty-handed. The fire of testing seemed to sweep away all of my religious doings. God did not want me to rest in these. For the future I was to forget all that I might ever do for God as quickly as it was accomplished, so that it might not prove a further snare to me, and go on as though I had never done a thing for God. This was my safety.

Without a doubt, even the least self-satisfaction in one's religious service is a great hindrance to the blessing and favor of God. It must be shunned as we would a serpent.

We continued to have wonderful meetings at Eighth and Maple. The Lord showed me He wanted this work to go deeper yet than anything we had experienced at that time. He was not satisfied fully with the Azusa work, deep as it had gone. There was still too much of the self-life, the religious self, among us. This naturally meant war, hard and bitter, against the Enemy. Ours was to be a sort of "clearing station," where fleshly exercises, false manifestations, and the religious self in general should be dealt with. We were after real experience, permanent and established, with Godlike character and no relapses.

I was greatly tested financially again. One day I had to walk twenty-five blocks to town, not having even carfare. A brother almost as poor as myself gave me a nickel to ride home. At the same time we were having glorious meetings. Many were prostrated under the power.

The Devil sent two strong characters one night to sidetrack the work. A spiritualist woman put herself at the head, like a drum major, to lead the singing. I prayed her out of the church. The other was a fanatical preacher with a voice that almost rattled the windows. I had to rebuke him openly. He had taken over the whole meeting. Conceit fairly stuck out of him. The Spirit was terribly grieved; God could not work. I had suffered too much for the work to turn things over to the Devil so easily. Besides, I was responsible for souls and for the rent.

We had a fierce battle with such spirits. They would have ruined everything. The Devil has no conscience, and the "flesh" has no sense. The very first time I opened the church for meetings, I found one of the worst fanatics and religious crooks in town sitting on the steps waiting for me. He was a preacher and wanted to run things. I chased him from the place like Nehemiah did the son of Joiada (Nehemiah 13:28). I had never dreamed there was so much of the Devil in so many people. The town seemed full of them. He tempted the saints to fight and hindered the Spirit. These crooks and cranks were the first at the meeting. We had a great clearing-up time. There was much professional, religious quackery. Judgment had to *"begin at the house of God"* (1 Peter 4:17).

Luther was greatly troubled with willful, religious fanatics in his day. From the Wartburg, where he was then concealed, he wrote to Melancthon at Wittenberg, giving a test-stone for these fanatics: "Ask these prophets whether they have felt those spiritual torments, those creations of God—that death and hell—which accompany a real separation." When he returned to Wittenberg and they tried their sorcery on him, he met them with these crude words: "I slap your spirit on the snout!" They acted like devils at that challenge. But it broke their spell.

We were obliged to deal firmly with the extreme case, but in the main, the Spirit passed over and moved irregularities out of the way without further advertising them. Many have declared we cannot throw our meetings open today. But if that is true, then we must shut God out also. What we need is more of God to control the meetings. He must be left free to come forth at all costs. The saints themselves are too largely in confusion and rebellion. Through prayer and self-abasement, God will undertake for the meetings. This was the secret in the beginning. We held together in prayer, love, and unity, and no power could break this. But self must be burned out. Meetings must be controlled by way of the throne. A spiritual atmosphere must be created, through humility and prayer, that Satan cannot live in. And this we realized in the beginning. It was the very opposite of religious zeal and carnal, religious ambition. We knew nothing about present-day "pep" and "make it snappy" methods. That whole system is an illegitimate product, as far as Pentecost is concerned. It takes time to be holy. The world rushes on. It gets us nowhere with God.

One reason for the depth of the work at Azusa was the fact that the workers were not novices. They were largely called and prepared for years from the Holiness ranks and from the mission field, and so on. They had been burnt out, tried, and proven. They were largely seasoned veterans. They had walked with God and learned deeply of His Spirit. These were pioneers, "shock troops," Gideon's three hundred, to spread the fire around the world, just as the disciples had been prepared by Jesus. We have now taken on a *"mixed multitude"* (Exodus 12:38), and the seeds of apostasy have had time to work. *"First love"* has been largely lost (Revelation 2:4). The dog has *"turned to his own vomit again"* (2 Peter 2:22) in many cases—that is, to Babylonian doctrines and practices. An enfeebled mother can hardly be expected to bring forth healthy children.

The Spirit dealt so deeply, and the people were so hungry in the beginning, that the carnal, human spirit injected into the meetings was discerned easily. It was as though a stranger had broken into a private, select company. The presence was painfully noticeable. Men were after God. He was in His holy temple; earth (all that is human) must keep silence before Him (Habukkuk 2:20). It only caused grief and pain. Our tarrying and prayer rooms today are but a shadow of the former ones, too often a place to blow off steam in human enthusiasm, or to become mentally intoxicated, supposedly from the Holy Spirit. This should not be. It is simply fanaticism.

In the early days, the tarrying room was the first thought and provision for a Pentecostal mission. It was held sacred, a kind of holy ground. There was mutual consideration also. There men sought to become quiet from the activities of their own too active minds and spirits, to escape from the world for the time, and get alone with God. There was no noisy, wild spirit there. That, at least, could be done elsewhere. The claims and confusion of an exacting world were shut out. It was a sort of "city of refuge" from this sort of thing, a haven of rest, where God could be heard and talk to their souls. Men would spend hours in silence there, searching their own hearts in privacy and securing the mind of the Lord for future action. This sort of thing seems nearly impossible today amid present surroundings. We die out to self by coming into His presence. And this requires great quietness of spirit. We need a "holy of holies." What Jew of old would have dared to act in God's temple as we do today in the missions? It would have meant death to him. We are full of foolishness and fanatical self-assertion. Even the formal Catholics have more reverence on the whole than we.

Sunday, August 26, Pastor Pendleton and about forty of his members came into Eighth and Maple to worship with us. They had received the baptism and spoken in tongues in their church. The denomination had thrown them out of their own building for this "unpardonable" crime. When I heard the church was going to try Pendleton for heresy, I invited them to come in with us if they were thrown out. Two days later they were expelled and accepted my invitation. Brother Pendleton declared after this experience that he would never build another doctrinal roof over his head. He was determined to go on for God.

Multitudes are shut up in ecclesiastical systems, within sectarian boundaries, while God's great, free pasture lies out before them, only limited by the encircling Word of God. *"There shall be one fold, and one shepherd"* (John 10:16). Traditional theology, partial truth and revelation, soon become law. The conscience is utterly bound, like Chinese footbinding, shut up against further progress.

Sunday, September 9, was a wonderful day. Several were stretched out under the power for hours. The altar was full all day, with scarcely any cessation to the services. Several received the baptism. In those days we preached but little. The people were taken up with God. Brother Pendleton and I could generally be found lying full-length on the low platform on our faces, in prayer, during the services. It was almost impossible to stay off our faces in those days. The presence of the Lord was so real. And this condition lasted for a long time. We had but little to do with guiding the meetings. Everyone was looking to God alone. We felt almost like apologizing when we had to claim attention from the people for announcements. It was a continuous sweep of victory—God had their attention. At times the audience would be convulsed with penitence. God dealt deeply with sin in those days. It could not remain in the camp.

The New Testament Church had a split about this time. I was glad I had nothing to do with that. Brother Smale had forced the Spirit-baptized saints to the wall, having finally rejected their testimony. A brother, Elmer Fisher, then started another mission at 327 South Spring Street, known as the Upper Room Mission. Most of the white saints from Azusa went with him, with the Spirit-baptized ones from the New Testament Church. This later became for a time the strongest mission in town. Both Azusa and the New Testament Church had by this time largely failed God.

I soon after turned Eighth and Maple over to Brother Pendleton, as I was too worn out to continue longer in constant service in the meetings. I had been for a long time under constant strain in prayer and meetings and needed a rest and change.

In the beginning of the Pentecostal work, I became very much exercised in the Spirit that Jesus should not be slighted, "lost in the temple," by the exaltation of the Holy Spirit and of the gifts of the Spirit. There seemed to be a great danger of losing sight of the fact that Jesus was *"all, and in all"* (Colossians 3:11). I endeavored to keep Him as the central theme and figure before the people. Jesus will always be the center of our preaching. All comes through and in Him. The Holy Spirit is given to show the things of Christ. (See John 16:14.) The work of Calvary, the Atonement, must be the center of our consideration. The Holy Spirit never draws our attention from Christ to Himself, but rather reveals Christ in a fuller way. We are in the same danger today.

There is nothing deeper or higher than to know Christ. Everything is given by God to that end. The *"one Spirit"* (1 Corinthians 12:13) is given to that end. Christ is our salvation and our all. That we might know *"the breadth, and length, and depth, and height...*[of] *the love of Christ"* (Ephesians 3:18–19), having a *"spirit of wisdom and revelation in the knowledge of him"* (Ephesians 1:17). It was to know Him (Christ) for which Paul strove. I was led to suddenly present Jesus one night to the congregation at Eighth and Maple. They had been forgetting Him in their exaltation of the Holy Spirit and the gifts. Now I introduced Christ for their consideration. They were taken completely by surprise and convicted in a moment. God made me do it. Then they saw their mistake and danger. I was preaching Christ one night at this time, setting Him before them in His proper place, when the Spirit so witnessed of His pleasure that I was overpowered by His presence, falling helplessly to the floor under a mighty revelation of Jesus to my soul. I fell, like John on the Isle of Patmos, at His feet.

I wrote a tract at this time, of which the following are extracts:

> We may not even hold a doctrine, or seek an experience, except in Christ. Many are willing to seek power from every battery they can lay their hands on in order to perform miracles and draw the attention and adoration of the people to themselves, thus robbing Christ of His glory and making a fair showing in the flesh. The greatest religious need of our day would seem to be that of true followers of the meek and lowly Jesus. Religious enthusiasm easily goes to seed. The human spirit so predominates the show-off, religious spirit. But we must stick to our text—Christ. He alone can save. The attention of the people must be first of all, and always, held to Him. A true Pentecost will produce a mighty conviction for sin, a turning to God. False manifestations produce only excitement and wonder. Sin and self-life will not materially suffer from these. We must get what our conviction calls for. Believe in your own heart's hunger and go ahead with God. Don't allow the Devil to rob you of a real Pentecost. Any work that exalts the Holy Spirit or the gifts above Jesus will finally end up in fanaticism. Whatever causes us to exalt and love Jesus is well and safe.

The reverse will ruin all. The Holy Spirit is a great light, but will always be focused on Jesus for His revealing.

A. S. Worrell, translator of the New Testament, was an earnest friend of Pentecost and a seeker after the baptism. He wrote the following in the *Way of Faith:*

The blood of Jesus is exalted in these meetings as I have rarely known elsewhere. There is a mighty power manifest in witnessing for Jesus, with a wonderful love for souls. There is also a bestowal of gifts of the Spirit. The places of meeting are at Azusa Street, at the New Testament Church, where Joseph Smale is pastor (some of his people were among the first to speak with tongues, but most have withdrawn because they felt restraint in his church), and at Eighth and Maple Streets, where Pastors Bartleman and Pendleton are the principal leaders.

In September 1906, the following letters appeared in the *Way of Faith,* from the pen of Dr. W. C. Dumble of Toronto, Canada, who was visiting Los Angeles at this time:

Possibly some of your readers may be interested in the impressions of a stranger in Los Angeles. A similar gracious work of the Spirit to that in Wales is in progress here. But while that is mostly in the churches, this is outside. The churches will not have it, or up to the present have stood aloof in a critical and condemnatory spirit. Like the work in Wales, this is a laymen's revival, conducted by the Holy Spirit and carried on in halls and old tumble-down buildings, whatever can be gotten for the work.

This is a remarkable movement, that may be said to be peculiar by the appearance of the gift of tongues. There are three different missions where one may hear these strange tongues. I had the rare joy of spending last evening at Pastor Bartleman's meeting, or more correctly, at a meeting where he and Pastor Pendleton are the nominal leaders, but where the Holy Spirit is actually in control. Jesus is proclaimed the Head, and the Holy Spirit His executive. Hence, there is no preaching, no choir, no organ, no collection, except what is voluntarily placed on the table or put in the box on the wall.

God was mightily present last night. Someone begins to sing: three or four hymns may be sung, interspersed with hallelujahs and amens. Then some overburdened soul rises and shouts, "Glory to Jesus!" and amid sobs and tears tells of a great struggle and a great deliverance. Then three or four are on the floor with shining faces. One begins to praise God and then breaks out with uplifted hands into a tongue. Pastor Pendleton now tells how he felt the need, and sought the baptism, and God baptized him with such an experience of the divine presence and love and boldness as he had never had before. The officials of his church therefore desired him to withdraw, and a number of his people went with him and joined forces with Pastor Bartleman. Then a sweet-faced, old, German Lutheran lady told how she wondered when she heard the people praising God in tongues and began to pray to be baptized with the Spirit. After she had gone to bed, her mouth went off in a tongue, and she praised the Lord through the night to the amazement of her children.

Next, an exhortation in tongues comes from Pastor Bartleman's lips in great sweetness, and one after another make their way to the altar quickly, until the rail is filled with seekers. Whatever criticism may be said of this work, it is very evident that it is divinely endorsed and the Lord is adding to them daily such as are being saved (Acts 2:47). It is believed that this revival is but in its infancy and that we are in the evening of this dispensation. The burden of the tongues is, "Jesus is coming soon."

Dr. Dumble wrote again, for the same paper,

At Pastor Bartleman's church, meetings are held every night, all day Sundays, and all night every Friday. There is no order of services; they are expected to run in the divine order. The blessed Holy Spirit is the executive in charge. The leaders, or pastors, will be seen most of the time on their faces on the floor, or kneeling in the place where the pulpit commonly is, but there is neither pulpit, nor organ, nor choir.

A young lady, for the first time in one of these meetings, came under the power of the Spirit, and lay for half an hour with beaming face lost to all about her, beholding visions unutterable. Soon she began to say, "Glory! Glory to Jesus!" and spoke fluently in a strange tongue. On the last Sabbath, the meeting continued from early morning to midnight. There was no preaching, but prayer, testimony, praise, and exhortation.

It is a fact that, in the beginning, platforms and pulpits were as far as possible removed out of the way. We had no conscious need of them. Priest class and ecclesiastical abuse were entirely swept away. We were all brethren. All were free to obey God. He might speak through whom He would. He had poured out His Spirit *"on all flesh"* (Acts 2:17), even on His *"servants and...handmaidens"* (verse 18). We honored men for their God-given gifts and offices only. As the movement began to wane, platforms were built higher, coattails were worn longer, choirs were organized, and string bands came into existence to "jazz" the people. The kings came back once more to their thrones, restored to sovereignty. We were no longer brethren. Then the divisions multiplied. While Brother Seymour kept his head inside the old empty box in Azusa all was well. They later built a throne for him also. Now we have not one hierarchy, but many.

I wrote for another religious paper the following, in 1906:

Cursed with unbelief, we are struggling upward—with the utmost difficulty—for the restoration of that glorious light and power, once so bountifully bestowed on the church, but long since lost. Our eyes have been so long blinded by the darkness of unbelief into which we were plunged by the church's fall, that we fight the light, for our eyes are weak. So far had we fallen as a church that when Luther sought to restore the truth of justification by faith, it was fought and resisted by the church of his day as the utmost heresy, and men paid for it with their lives. And it was much the same in Wesley's time. Now, here we are with the restoration of the very experience of Pentecost—with the *"latter rain"* (James 5:7), a restoration of the power, in greater glory—to finish up the work begun. We shall yet again be lifted to the church's former level, to complete her work, begin where they left off when failure overtook them, and, speedily fulfilling the last Great Commission, open the way for the coming of the Christ.

We are to drop out the centuries of the church's failure, the long, dismal Dark Ages, and telescoping time, be now fully restored to pristine power, victory, and glory. We seek to pull ourselves, by the grace of God, out of a corrupt, backslidden, spurious Christianity. The synagogues of a proud, hypocritical church are arrayed against us, to give us the lie. The "hirelings" thirst for our blood. The scribes and Pharisees, chief priests, and rulers of the synagogues are all against us and the Christ.

Los Angeles seems to be the place and this the time, in the mind of God, for the restoration of the church to her former place, favor, and power. The fullness of time (Galatians 4:4) seems to have come for the church's complete restoration. God has spoken to His servants in all parts of the world and has sent many of them to Los Angeles, representing every nation under heaven. Once more, as of old, they are come up for Pentecost, to go out again into all the world with the glad message of salvation. The base of operations has been shifted, from old Jerusalem to Los Angeles for the latter Pentecost. And there is a tremendous, God-given hunger for this experience everywhere. Wales was but intended as the cradle for this worldwide restoration of the power of God. India but the Nazareth where He was "brought up."   —*Apostolic Light*

Again I wrote in the same paper,

If ever men shall seek to control, corner, or own this work of God, either for their own glory or for that of an organization, we shall find the Spirit refusing to work. The glory will depart. Let this be one work where God shall be given His proper place, and we shall see such a work as men have never yet dreamed of. It would be a fearful thing if God were obliged to withdraw His blessed Spirit from us, or withhold it at such a time as this, because we tried to corner it. All our business is to get God to the people. Let us yield ourselves for this, and this alone.

Some of the "canker worms" of past experience have been party spirit, sectional difference, prejudices, and so on, which are all carnal, contrary, and destructive to the law of love, to the *"one body"* of Christ (1 Corinthians 12:13). *"For by one Spirit are we all baptized into one body"* (verse 13). Self-satisfaction will always cause defeat. Oh, brother! Cease traveling round and round your old habit-beaten path, on which all grass has ceased to grow. Strike out into pastures green, beside the living waters!

In the *Way of Faith,* I wrote the following:

We are coming back from the "dark ages" of the church's backsliding and downfall. We are living in the most momentous moments of the history of time. The Spirit is brushing aside all our plans, our schemes, our strivings, and our theories, and is Himself acting again. Many who have feathered their nests well are fighting hard. They cannot face the sacrifice involved in rising to meet these conditions.

The precious ore of truth, the church's emancipation from the bondage of man's rule, has been brought about in a necessarily crude form at first, as rough ore. It has been surrounded, as in nature, by all kinds of worthless, hurtful elements. Extravagant, violent characters have sought to identify themselves with the work. A great truth is struggling in the bowels of the earth, entombed by the landslide of retrograding evil in the church's history. But it is bursting forth, soon to shake itself free from the objectionable matter yet clinging to it. Christ is at last proclaimed the Head. The Holy Spirit is the life. The members are in principle all *"one body"* (1 Corinthians 12:13).

Again, some extracts from an article in the *Way of Faith* in early 1907:

We detect in these present-hour manifestations the rising of a new order of things out of the chaos and failure of the past. The atmosphere is filled with inspiring expectation of the ideal. But unbelief retards our progress. Our preconceived ideas betray us in the face of opportunity. They lead to loss and ruin. But the world is awakening today, startled from her guilty slumber of ease and death. Letters are pouring in from every side, from all parts of the world, inquiring feverishly, *"What meaneth this?"* (Acts 2:12). Ah, we have the pulse of humanity, especially in the church of today. There is a mighty expectation. And these hungry, expectant children are crying for bread. Cold, intellectual speculation has had nothing but denials for them. The realm of the Spirit cannot be reached alone by the intellect. The miraculous has again startled us into a realization of the fact that God still lives and moves among us.

Old forms are breaking up, passing away. Their death knell is being sounded. New forms, a new order and life, are appearing. There is naturally a mighty struggle. Satan moves the hosts of hell to hinder. But we shall conquer! The precious ore must be refined after it has been mined. The *"precious"* must be taken *"from the vile"* (Jeremiah 15:19). Rough pioneers have cleared the way for our advance, but purer forms will follow. Heroic, positive spirits are necessary for this work.

Men have been speaking through the ages, but the voice of God the Spirit is calling us today. Since the early church lost her power and place with God, we have been struggling back. Up through "its" and "isms," theories, creeds, doctrines, schisms, issues, movements, blessings, experiences, and professions, we have come. The stream could rise no higher than its source. We need no more theology or theory. Let the Devil have them. Let us get to God. Many are cramped up in present experiences.

They are actually afraid to seek more of God for fear the Devil will get them. Away with such foolish bondage! Follow your heart! Believe in your own heart's hunger, and go ahead for God. We are sticking to the bottom. We need the fire of God. Straightjacket methods and religious rules have nearly crushed out our spiritual life altogether. We had better grieve all men rather than God.

Before the Azusa outpouring, everything had settled down in concrete form, bound by man. Nothing could move for God. Dynamite—the power of the Holy Spirit—was necessary to free this mass. And this God furnished. The whole mass was set free once more. Our Year of Jublilee had come. The last one had been realized in the great revival of 1859, fifty years before.

Chapter 4

Traveling Ministry

The latter part of March 1907, I received an invitation to come to Conneaut, Ohio, with a check enclosed for fifty dollars. They wanted Pentecostal meetings there. The leader wrote me that they were hungry for Pentecost. I felt it was a call from God to go east but could not help wondering if they really knew what they were inviting for themselves. The letter seemed full of enthusiasm, the very thing John Wesley so strongly discouraged. Wesley's definition of fanaticism was, "expecting the end without the means."

I did not cash the check, fearing lest they might be disappointed when they got through with me. They had to learn that Pentecost meant the dying out to the self-life, carnal ambition, pride, and so on. It meant for them to enter into the *"fellowship of his sufferings"* (Philippians 3:10), not simply to have a popular, good time. This I felt they did not realize. A real Christian means a martyr, unavoidably, in one way or another. Few people are willing to pay the price to become a real Christian, to accept the ostracism, false accusation, and condemnation of others. But God has only one standard. Present-day profession of faith is for the most part a mere sham. Only a small percentage of it is real.

A man once asked Luther to recommend a book that was both agreeable and useful. "Agreeable and useful!" replied Luther. "Such a question is beyond my ability. The better things are, the less they please."

"Except a man forsake all," said Jesus, "he cannot be my disciple." (See Luke 14:33.) This may require some qualification, or explanation, as to positive action, but the principle remains the same for all. The church, since her fall in the early centuries, has had an altogether mistaken idea of her calling and salvation. All believers are called to a 100 percent consecration. God doesn't have two standards of consecration—one for the foreign missionary, and another for the Christian at home. We cannot find it in the Bible. One is called to consecrate his all as well as the other, as God's stewards in their own places and callings. It takes three to make a missionary. One goes, one prays, and one gives. *This is a hard saying; who can hear it?* (John 6:60).

God has had but one purpose and interest since the Fall. That has been to bring man back to Himself. The whole old dispensation, with its providential dealings, was unto this one end. God had one recognized people, the Jews. He had one purpose in this nation. All their operations were to one end. All their worship pointed to that one end—to bring the nations to the true knowledge of God and to bring in the Messiah of the world. Jesus Christ had but one interest in coming to this earth. His second coming waits for this one thing also. When this Gospel shall have been preached in all the world, *"then shall the end come"* (Matthew 24:14) and the curse be lifted.

Is the church working, with all her resources, for this one purpose and to this one end? That certainly does not mean the selfish heaping up of property and riches, more than we really need. It does not mean getting all we want for ourselves and then tossing the Lord a dollar we do not need. We have had the order totally reversed since the early church's fall. God requires of everyone exactly the same consecration.

Here is where the Ananias and Sapphira business has come in. Not "one-tenth" in this dispensation, but "all." Our bodies are the temple of the Holy Spirit (1 Corinthians 6:19), and we are to be 100 percent for Him at all times. We belong to Him. He has created us and bought us back, redeemed us after we had mortgaged His property, not ours, to the Devil. In no sense are we our own. We are redeemed back with the blood. How long would it take, or have taken, to evangelize the world under this rule? Think on these things! Is the church moving normally, in divine order? The politico-religious system, since the early church, and today, is largely a hybrid, mongrel institution. It is full of selfishness, disobedience, and corruption. Its kingdom has become "of this world," rather than a "heavenly citizenship," with spiritual weapons.

The doctrinal issue has also been a great battle. Many were too dogmatic at Azusa. Doctrine, after all, is but the skeleton of the structure. It is the framework of the "body." We need flesh on the bones, the Spirit within, to give life. What the people need is a living Christ, not dogmatic, doctrinal contention. Much harm was done to the work in the beginning by unwise zeal. The cause suffered most from those within its own ranks, as always. But God had some real heroes He could depend upon. Most of these sprang from the deepest obscurity into sudden prominence and power, and then as quickly retired again, when their work was done. Someone has well said, "Men, like stars, appear on the horizon at the command of God." This is a true evidence of a real work of God. Men do not make their times, as someone has also truly said, but the times make the man. Until the time, no man can produce a revival. The people must be prepared, and the instrument likewise.

The historian D'Aubigne has well said,

> God draws from the deepest seclusion the weak instruments by which He purposes to accomplish great things; and then, when He has permitted them to glitter for a season with dazzling brilliancy on an illustrious stage, he dismisses them again to deepest obscurity. God usually withdraws His servants from the field of battle only to bring them back stronger and better armed.

And this was the case with Luther, shut up in the Wartburg, after his glittering triumph over the great ones of earth at Worms.

D'Aubigne wrote,

> There is a moment in the history of the world, as in the lives of such men as Charles II

or Napoleon, which decides their career and their renown. It is that in which their strength is suddenly revealed to them. An analogous moment exists in the life of God's heroes, but it is in a contrary direction. It is that in which they first recognize their helplessness and nothingness. From that hour they receive the strength of God from on high. A great work of God is never accomplished by the natural strength of man. It is from among the dry bones, the darkness, and the dust of death that God is pleased to select the instruments through whom He designs to scatter over the earth His light, regeneration, and life.

Strong in frame, in character, and in talents, Zwingle had to see himself prostrated, so that he might become such an instrument as God loves. He needed the baptism of adversity and infirmity, of weakness and pain. Luther had received it in that hour of anguish when his cell and the long galleries of the convent at Erfurth reechoed with his piercing cries. Zwingle was appointed to receive it by being brought into contact with sickness and death.

Men must come to know their own weakness before they can hope to know God's strength. The natural strength and ability of man are always the greatest hindrance to the work of God, and to God's working. That is why we had such a deep dying out, especially for the workers and preachers, in the early days of the Azusa Mission. God was preparing His workers for their mission.

In answer to prayer, the Lord opened the way for me to take my family with me when I went east. I preached in Denver at the Holiness headquarters, where we had been members and labored before we had come to California. We had a powerful time. Several souls were saved, among them one whole family, and the saints were wonderfully built up. Some received the baptism of the Spirit. I had three meetings in all.

God wonderfully used two little girls there. They both had the baptism and a real ministry of prayer. Their pleadings with the unsaved broke up the house, while their freedom from self-consciousness was a powerful lesson to us all. It was a strange work and ministry of God. Heartfelt conviction was upon the unsaved. "Unless you become as a little child," we learned anew. (See Mark 10:14.) Evidently modern evangelistic methods are not altogether essential for the salvation of souls. We had better stick to our peculiar gift, though it be a *"strange work"* (Isaiah 28:21). We will succeed better at that. Let God have His way. In those days the power and presence of God among us often converted sinners in their seats. We did not have to drag them to the altar and fight with them to get them saved. They did not come to the altar to fight God. There was much of the "singing in the Spirit" at Denver, as at Azusa. This gift seemed to accompany the work wherever it broke out.

We finally reached Conneaut, Ohio, on April 30 in a snowstorm. The presence of the Lord was with us from the start. It was a Holiness mission. We really had little to do but to look on and see God work. The Spirit took the meetings. In fact, we were on our faces most of the time in prayer. I could hardly keep off my face; the battle was the Lord's. And no one else could have fought it there, for we came up against most stubborn resistance. The Lord had warned me of this condition before we left Los Angeles. The leader who had written inviting me had not the slightest idea what Pentecost meant, just as I had feared. He wanted a good time, with a big increase in the mission, to build up the work in numbers, and so on.

The meetings had not gone far until we found him wedged squarely in the way. One sister prayed without ceasing under a travail of soul for him. He was fleshly, proud, and self-important, and would not let the meetings go deeper. We could go no further. He did not seem to have the least idea of humbling himself along with the rest of us. But he had to come down. God showed me I must deal with him. I had to obey or quit. There was no use going any further. We were eating at his table and sleeping in his beds. It was a hard thing to have to do, but I went after him. We locked horns, and he resisted me fiercely. God, however, brought him down. The Spirit convinced him, and he fell in a heap. He almost jarred the building when he fell. He lay under a bench for five hours and began to see himself as God saw him. The Spirit took him all to pieces and showed him his pride, ambition, and so on. Finally, he got up without a word and went home. There he locked himself in his room and remained until God met him. He came out from that interview as meek as a little lamb and confessed his shortcomings. The hindrance was out of the way, and the meetings swept on in power. He got the baptism himself some time later, after we had gone.

The Lord worked very deeply. Several were under the power all night on one occasion. There was no closing at 9 o'clock sharp, as the preachers must do in order to keep the people. We wanted God in those days. We did not have a thousand other things we wanted before Him. And He did not disappoint us. One sister sat and spoke in tongues for five full hours. Souls were saved, and the saints wonderfully built up and strengthened by the presence of the Lord. A number received the baptism in the Spirit, and the mission became full-fledged for Pentecost.

One Sunday night the hall was packed, clear out to the middle of the street. I went to the hall the next morning to look for the folks who had not gone home. Several had stayed all night. I found them lost to all but God. They could not get away. A very Shekinah glory filled the place. It was awesome, but glorious.

Our next meeting was at Youngstown, Ohio. Here I preached for the Christian Missionary Alliance (C.M.A.). Some nights we were held in the hall until daylight. We could not leave. God was so near that no one felt tired or sleepy. I had much real soul travail here. In some meetings suppressed groans were about all one could hear. Much prayer characterized the services. The Spirit was waited upon for every move, and He took complete control. No two services were alike. In one meeting, the very silence of heaven took possession of us for about four hours. Scarcely a sound was uttered. The place became so steeped in prayer and so sacred that we closed the door softly, and walked the same, scarcely speaking to one another, and then only in whispers. Another night, we were held in adoration and praise for hours. We seemed to be looking into the very face of God. There was no boisterousness in these meetings.

Another night we were all broken up by the love of God. We could do nothing but weep for a whole hour.

Every meeting was different, and each seemed to go deeper. Two or three whole nights were spent in prayer. One night the Spirit fell upon us like an electric shower. Several went over on the floor, and God was Master for the time. Such singing in the Spirit, the "heavenly chorus," I have seldom heard. A number came through speaking in tongues. But again our battle was with the leader. He opposed me fiercely. He was not right with God and would not yield. His wife was now under the power, seeking the baptism, but he carried on in the flesh until the Spirit was terribly grieved. The Devil often gets into a preacher's coat. Satan used him persistently in the beginning of the meetings, but God finally got the victory, in spite of him. He did not yield. It is amazing the hold the Devil has on some preachers.

I preached one night at Akron, Ohio, with much blessing. We then had five services at New Castle, Pennsylvania, with the C.M.A. again. God greatly blessed there also. Then we went to Alliance, Ohio, for the Pentecostal camp meeting. It was June 13. We had a wonderful camp. It was the first one of its kind in the Northeast. I led the preachers' meetings. The first Sunday morning I was given a message, but the leader asked me to speak in the afternoon instead. I said nothing, but prayed. In a few minutes he came back and told me to preach in the morning. In those days men did not get far without God. I preached with great help from the Lord on, "Jesus Christ in Worldwide Evangelism in the Power of the Holy Ghost." Everything centers around Jesus. We may not put the power, gifts, the Holy Spirit, or in fact anything ahead of Jesus. Any mission that exalts even the Holy Spirit above the Lord Jesus Christ is bound for the rocks of error and fanaticism.

This was a very important camp in the inception of the work in that part of the country. We remained two weeks, and I preached eleven times in all. We had a powerful time and a large, representative attendance. Four hundred camped on the grounds. Often meetings lasted all night. Missionary enthusiasm ran high. Meals were on the free-will offering plan. God bountifully provided and a precious spirit of unity prevailed. We were brethren, baptized *"by one Spirit...into one body"* (1 Corinthians 12:13). Thus Jesus' prayer was answered, *"That they all may be one"* (John 17:21). The harmony between the preachers was especially blessed. Such a spirit of love we have seldom seen displayed. Those were wonderful days. It could be truly said that in honor we preferred one another (Romans 12:10).

No organ or hymnals were used. The Spirit conducted the services, and there seemed no place for them. Hundreds met God. Many received a call to foreign fields, to prove God along real faith lines. The rapid evangelism of the world, on real apostolic lines, was the goal set. The present generation must be reached by the present generation. The altars were seldom empty of seekers day or night. Men who had been in both the Wales and India revivals declared this to be the deepest work of all. We determined to fight nothing but sin and to fear nothing but God.

I asked the Lord for a certain amount of money, which we needed in order to continue east. The committee gave me exactly the amount I had prayed for, without a single hint from me. God did it. Praise Him!

At Forty-second Street Mission, New York City (Glad Tidings Hall), we had powerful times. A young girl came under the power, and her spirit was caught up to the throne. She sang a melody, without words, that was so heavenly that it seemed to come from within the veil. It seemed to come from another world. I have never heard its equal before or since.

A. B. Simpson was there himself that night and was tremendously impressed by it. He had been much opposed to the Pentecostal work. Doubtless God gave it as a witness for him. Several were slain under the power. Toward morning, the presence of the Lord was simply wonderful. I went to leave the hall just at day-break and shook hands with a sister hungry for the baptism. The Spirit came upon her, and I could not turn her loose until she fell at the altar and came through speaking in tongues. I shook hands with another hungry sister as I started to leave the hall again. The Spirit fell upon her also, and she received the baptism right there on her feet, speaking in tongues before I could turn her loose. That was a wonderful night.

It was now time for us to start for California again. The Lord had blessed me much at Indianapolis. I was so glad I had obeyed Him and gone there. I was there by His invitation purely, but I seldom, if ever, had felt such a wonderful flow of the Spirit before. The message seemed to be actually pulled out of me in preaching. In fact, I felt almost drawn off the platform by the hungry desire of the people. I could not talk as rapidly as the thoughts came to me and almost fell over myself trying to speak fast enough. At one meeting, when I was through speaking, the *"slain of the LORD"* (Isaiah 66:16) lay all over the floor. I looked for the preachers behind me, and they lay stretched out on the floor, too. One of them had his feet tangled up in a chair, so I knew they had gone down under the power of God. I stepped over near the piano, among the people. My body began to rock under the power of God, and I fell over onto the piano and lay there. It was a cyclonic manifestation of the power of God.

At Colorado Springs I preached six times. The Spirit flowed like oil. I have seldom found such liberty anywhere. Oh, the possibilities that exist where purity and unity reign!

We had sent our trunks on to Los Angeles, not knowing where we would find our next home. But before reaching Pasadena, the Lord showed me we should get off there. We did not expect anyone to meet us, though I had written Brother Boehmer that we would get back on that train. When we reached Pasadena, with no place to go, we found Brother Boehmer at the depot waiting for us. He took us to a mission home on Mary Street that had just been opened in connection with the Alley Mission. So God had it all arranged for us, without our knowledge. We were weary pilgrims indeed, needing rest. We arrived December 5, 1907.

I found the work had fallen back considerably. The saints were badly split up. The Spirit was bound also. The outside opposition had become much more settled and determined. It was the same condition in Los Angeles. The saints at the Alley Mission had suffered greatly under the tyranny of a leader who did not himself have the baptism. I now helped them to pray him out of the mission and the home, and they were delivered. He had imposed himself on the work. He was a regular "dog in the manger." A larger mission was opened on Colorado Street, and I had some ministry there also. I found the power had been greatly dissipated. There was much empty manifestation. A great deal of it was simply froth and foam. This burdened me deeply. The spirit of prayer had been largely lost. In consequence, much flesh and fanaticism had crept in. Prayer burns out the proud flesh. It must be crucified.

We now moved into a little cottage next door to Brother Boehmer. The ministry of intercession was heavy upon me. I preached a number of times at Hermon, Eighth and Maple, and Azusa Street. One evening at Azusa Mission the spirit of prayer came upon me as *"a rushing mighty wind"* (Acts 2:2). The power ran all through the building. I had been burdened for the deadness that had crept in there. The temporary leaders were frightened and did not know what to do. They telephoned for help. They had not been with us in the beginning. Brother Seymour was out of town.

I was upstairs in the hallway. Others joined me in prayer. We went downstairs, and the fire broke out in the meeting. But the leaders in charge were not spiritual. Other rulers had arisen that *"knew not Joseph"* (Exodus 1:8). They did not understand it. God was trying to come back. They seemed afraid someone might steal the mission. The Spirit could not work. Besides, they had organized now, and I had not joined their organization. And so it is largely today: "Sign on the dotted line or we cannot trust you. We affiliate only with those carrying our papers." Pentecost took that out of us! Why go back to it? All who belong to the different divisions in the Pentecostal work today do not have the spirit of division, but God would hold us to the ideal of the "one body."

113

The Lord showed me my place of hiding. I determined to follow Him. That is the place of power. Fear nothing but God, and obey Him. I spoke many times at Eighth and Maple, at Azusa, and also at the Alley Mission in Pasadena, exhorting them to more earnestness and to walk in the Spirit. I had suffered much in prayer in the bringing forth of this work and felt I had a right to admonish them. Our great battle from the beginning was with fleshly religious fanatics, purporting to be of the Spirit of God.

On March 11, 1908, I received a letter from Brother Sawtelle, leader of the Christian Alliance work in Portland, Oregon. He asked me to come north and hold some meetings for them. God had shown me that we would be called out again, and I recognized His call. We were to go north and east again. Brother Boehmer had received the baptism by this time and decided to go with us in the work. I felt we had come back to the coast largely to get him out.

I was exhorting the saints all winter to push out in the spring for God. About a dozen followed us to different points as we started out again. I began to feel the worldwide call heavily upon me, also. The Lord seemed to show me the oceans must yet be crossed for Him. And this we realized later on. Like Peter the Hermit,* I felt at times like stirring all Christendom with my cry for a revival.

[Brother Bartleman spent the year of 1908 ministering again throughout the United States. In 1909 he made a trip to the Hawaiian Islands.—Editor]

---

* Peter the Hermit, born about 1050 in France, was the founder of a monastery and is considered one of the chief stimulators of the launching of the First Crusade.

The work had gotten into a bad condition generally by the time we returned to Los Angeles (from the Hawaiian Islands). The missions had fought each other almost to a standstill. Little love remained. There was considerable rejoicing, but all in the flesh. A cold, hardhearted zeal had largely taken the place of the divine love and tenderness of the Spirit. The missions, I found, were very zealous for doctrine, as usual. I began to preach at Eighth and Maple, Azusa Mission, and Hermon. Azusa had lost out greatly since we left. *"How are the mighty fallen"* (2 Samuel 1:19) came to me most forcibly. But the Spirit came upon three of us mightily in prayer one evening there. He assured us He was going to bring the power back to Azusa Mission again as at the beginning. We felt we had prayed through. (And the answer came a little over a year later when Brother Durham came from Chicago. The place was then once more filled with the saints and with the glory of God, although only for a short time.)

But at this time old Azusa Mission fell more and more into bondage. The meetings had to run in appointed order. The Spirit tried to work through some poor, illiterate Mexicans, who had been saved and baptized in the Spirit, but the leader deliberately refused to let them testify, crushing them ruthlessly. It was like murdering the Spirit of God. Only God knows what this meant to those poor Mexicans. Personally, I would rather die than to have assumed such a spirit of dictatorship. Every meeting was now programmed from start to finish. Disaster was bound to follow, and it did so.

I now began to feel the Lord was calling me to girdle the globe on a missionary trip for Him. It was to be by faith, and I had not a cent in sight. I had really felt the call to make this trip for years, and the time had now come. It looked like madness to attempt such a thing in the natural, as I was just at that time up against a very severe test both physically and financially. However, the conviction became an assurance. After a time, in which it seemed almost impossible to get even as much as a dime, the Lord opened the way for me to start. I believe God allowed me to be thus tested in order to prove me for the journey. It looked almost like actual starvation faced us just before the way finally opened up.

I left home March 17, 1910, and circled the entire globe by faith, visiting Europe and most of the principal mission fields. I spent six delightful weeks in Palestine, returning home by way of Egypt, India, Ceylon, China, and Japan, and across the Pacific, via Honolulu. I was gone eleven months and one week. My family trusted God fully and were better cared for than they had ever been while I was with them. I returned with about one dollar in my pocket. My wife had fifty dollars in the bank. *"Faithful is he that calleth you, who also will do it"* (1 Thessalonians 5:24).

Chapter 5

The Wave Continues

Just about one week before I arrived home, Brother Durham began meetings at old Azusa Mission. He was sent by the Lord from Chicago. The Upper Room Mission refused him a hearing, so he went to Azusa Street. Brother Seymour was absent, having traveled east. Brother Durham started meetings, and the saints flocked back to the old place and filled it again with the high praises of God. This was what the Lord witnessed to three of us while in prayer more than a year before. God had gathered many of the old Azusa workers back to Los Angeles from many parts of the world, evidently for this. It was called by many the second shower of the *"latter rain"* (James 5:7). On Sunday the place was crowded, and five hundred were turned away. The people would not leave their seats between meetings for fear of losing them.

With this, the bottom dropped out of Upper Room Mission overnight. The leader had abused his privilege, and also the saints. He had failed God in other ways also. The Lord will spare any man or mission if there is repentance. We cannot persistently abuse our privileges, destroy the prophets of God, and finally get away with it. Great was the fall of Upper Room Mission. The leader had at one time been much used by God, but God had another place, man, and message ready. He never deserts His true flock. The "cloud" moved on and moved the saints with it. (See Exodus 13:21–22.)

The fire began to fall at old Azusa as at the beginning. I attended these meetings with great interest and joy. The Lord also blessed me much at Eighth and Maple, which was still running in spite of the outstanding meetings at Azusa.

Then, on May 2, I went to Azusa Street and to everyone's surprise found the doors all locked, with chain and padlock. Brother Seymour had hastened back from the east and, with his trustees, decided to lock Brother Durham out. It was his message they objected to. But they locked God and the saints out from the old cradle of power also.

In a few days, Brother Durham rented a large building at the corner of Seventh and Los Angeles Streets. A thousand people attended the meetings there on Sundays and about four hundred on weeknights. Here the "cloud" rested, and God's glory filled the place. Azusa became deserted. The Lord was with Brother Durham in great power, for God sets His seal especially on *"present truth"* (2 Peter 1:12) that needs to be established. He preached a Gospel of salvation by faith and was used mightily to draw anew a clear line of demarcation between salvation by works and faith, between law and grace. This had become very much needed, and it is certain that such a revelation and reformation are needed in the churches today almost as badly as in Luther's day.

"Learn from me," said Luther, "how difficult a thing it is to throw off errors which have been confirmed by the example of all the world, and which, through long habit, have become second nature to us."

"Men were astonished that they had not earlier acknowledged truths that appeared so evident in Luther's mouth," said the historian D'Aubigne. And so with Durham's message. But it received great opposition also. Some abused the message, as they do every message sent by God, going to the extreme of declaring that because the work of redemption was fully accomplished on the cross, it was of necessity finished in us also, the moment we believed. This was a great error and hindered the message and work considerably.

Man always adds to the message God has given. This is Satan's chief way to discredit and destroy it. Both Luther and Wesley had the same difficulties to contend with. And so has every God-given revival. Men are creatures of extremes. The message generally suffers more from its friends than from its foes. *"We have this treasure in earthen vessels"* (2 Corinthians 4:7). The truth can always be abused. Some even went so far as to fight the principle of holiness itself, pretending to justify themselves by Durham's message. But they had either misunderstood it or, what is more likely, seized a pretended opportunity to fight the principle that their own hearts refused to yield to.

We had a wonderful year in Los Angeles in 1911. The battle was clearly between works and faith, between law and grace. Much of the old-time power and glory of the Azusa Mission days returned to us. I had much liberty and joy in Brother Durham's mission, especially in the beginning. God had prepared me beforehand for the message. I had been brought completely to the end of self-dependence. Works had no further place with me in meriting any phase of salvation. *"For we are his workmanship, created in Christ Jesus unto good works"* (Ephesians 2:10). We were called to humility again, so that the power of God might rest upon us.

So determined was I to take no chances of "self" surviving in my life that I burned no less than five hundred personal letters I had received in the early Azusa days from leading preachers and teachers all over the world inquiring anxiously about the revival that was then in our midst. Some of these inquirers were in very high positions officially. They had read my reports of the revival in various papers. I was afraid these letters might someday prove a temptation to me to imagine that I had been a person of some importance, since many begged an interest in my prayers. I almost wish at times that I had kept these letters, as they would be of much interest now as historical evidence to the widespread influence of the revival. No doubt the Lord could have kept me humble without this sacrifice, but at the time I was determined to take no chances.

We feared nothing more in those days than to seek our own glory, or that the Pentecostal experience would become a matter of past history. In fact, we hoped and believed that the revival would last without cessation until Jesus should come. It doubtless would, and should, if men would not fail God, but we drift back continually into the old ecclesiastical concepts, forms, and ceremonies. Thus history sadly repeats itself. Now we must work up an annual revival. We go to church on Sundays, just like the nations (churches) round about us. (See Deuteronomy 17:14.) But in the beginning it was not so. In the early Azusa days, you could hardly keep the saints off their knees. Whenever two believers met, they invariably went to prayer. Today we can hardly be dragged to prayer. Some make as much fuss about it as the old camel does in the East in kneeling to receive his load. He fusses and bites and groans before the driver can bring him down.

I am glad I did not destroy my diary, however, or the articles I wrote all through those early Pentecostal days. I have preserved between five and six hundred separate, printed articles, besides more than one hundred different tracts. From these I have been able to draw a large amount of most reliable information for the present book. Had I destroyed these, this book would probably never have been written.

The opposition against Brother Durham was tremendous, and he was finally tempted to strike back. This I felt was not the Spirit of Christ, though he had great provocation. Possibly few have been able to stand such a test successfully. I left the platform finally, not willing to stand for a spirit of retaliation. I felt I must keep clear of carnal strife and controversy. However, the Lord had wonderfully used dear Brother Durham. He was sent by God to Los Angeles, and possibly his work was done. To have remained much

longer might have destroyed his victory, for his word
was coming to be almost law in the Pentecostal missions, even as far as the Atlantic coast. Too much
power is unsafe for any one man. The paper he instituted in connection with his work began to take on the
nature of a carnal controversy, fighting the old "second work of grace" theory. The Lord showed me He
was about to stop this spirit.

Brother Durham wrote the following observations
on the work some time before he died. They are of
such vital importance I feel led to reproduce them, as
follows:

> A great crisis is now on. Men do not see the
> plan of God in the present Pentecostal Move-
> ment. Such a complete revolution is necessary
> that it staggers them. They are unwilling to see
> that which they have labored so hard to build
> up thrown down; but before God's plans can be
> carried out, man's plans must be set aside. They
> fail to see that God, having set aside all the
> plans of man, is beginning to work after His
> own plan. He is revealing His real plan to so
> many that they will never consent to having the
> present work turned into a sect. God's people
> are simply not going to be led into the snare of
> human organization again.

> The Father has poured out His Spirit again
> so that Jesus may be glorified. All past move-
> ments have resulted in the promotion to posi-
> tions of honor for one or more men. The
> present movement will honor and exalt Jesus
> Christ. The Holy Spirit always exalts Jesus and
> His precious blood. As He is exalted and faith-
> fully preached, God is restoring the old-time

power. But it is not all restored yet. Not seeing the plan of God, men have not met the conditions and therefore have not received all that God has for them. Many have run ahead of God.

Shortly after God filled me, His Spirit rested mightily upon me one morning, and He said to me, "If you were only small enough, I could do anything with you." A great desire to be little, yea, to be nothing, came into my heart. But it has been oh so hard to keep low enough for Him to really work through me. And He only really uses me when I am little in my own eyes and really humble at His feet. When I feel that I must do something, He always lets me fail. But when I stay at His feet and feel that I am nothing, and that He is all, and so just trust Him, He does His work in such a beautiful way that it is wonderful to me.

God is not trying to build up something else, or to do something for men that will make them great and mighty, but rather to bring all men to nothing and to do the work through the power of the Holy Ghost. The call of God to His people now is to humble themselves, to recognize their weakness and lack of power, to get down before Him and wait till His power is restored. The great question is, Will men see the plan of God and yield to it? Will men get down in humility at Jesus' feet and pray and wait till He restores His full Pentecostal power? Or will they continue to run ahead of Him and fail in the end?

Let God's people everywhere begin to seek in deep, true humility. Then He will reveal Himself and His plan to them. One man with the real power of God upon him can do more than a thousand who go on their own account. Only those who are true and loyal to God and His present-day message will share in this great victory. The people who really humble themselves and stand the test, God will use to do His work.

The fact is when a man gets to the place where he really loves obscurity, where he does not care to preach, and where he would rather sit in the backseat than on the platform, then God can lift him up and use him, and not very much before.

The old Upper Room, 327 South Spring Street, was opened up again about this time under the leadership of Brother Warren Fisher, Brother Manley, and Brother Allen. I delivered a message there one Sunday, and two received the baptism of the Spirit. God wonderfully anointed me. The presence of the Lord was very near. I had asked Him for a witness, so I now shifted my ministry to the Upper Room Mission.

After I left Brother Durham's platform, he seemed to mistrust me. Perhaps he thought I would work against him. I spoke many times now at Upper Room Mission, where the Lord greatly blessed me. Soon after this, Brother Durham went to Chicago to hold a convention where he was wonderfully used by God. It was in the winter, and he contracted a cold that led to his death soon after returning to Los Angeles.

By this time, the Lord was speaking loudly to me about getting out into the field again. I felt strongly drawn to Europe. I had had conviction of this when passing through Europe in 1910. The time had come, and the Lord began to touch hearts in a marked way on our behalf.

We left Los Angeles and started to work our way across the continent once more, this time en route for Europe. The account of our "Two Years' Mission Work in Europe," with labors in England, Scotland, Wales, Holland, Switzerland, France, Germany, Norway, Sweden, Finland, and old Russia itself—where I had to preach in secret, although almost under the czar's nose—was published in a separate booklet. We did not want to return to America so soon, but were obliged to in safety to the family, because of the war. Besides, the whole effort of the nations now became one of filling their people's hearts with hate and murder. There seemed no place for the spirit of the Gospel. You are expected to do all you can to hate, curse, or kill the enemy in wartime, certainly not to love him. Let others do this, however, if they will; but as for me, the Gospel is just the same in peace or war. *"Jesus Christ the same yesterday, and to day, and for ever"* (Hebrews 13:8).

In all my writings, for at least twenty-five years, I have labored for the unity of the body of Christ. Everything I've written is full of the sentiment of John 17:21. Dr. Philip Schaff, the well-known scholar, has happily declared,

> The divisions of Christendom will finally be overruled for a deeper and richer harmony, of which Christ is the keynote. In Him and by Him all problems of theology and history will be solved. In the best case, a human creed is only an approximate and relatively correct expression of revealed truth and may be improved by the progressive knowledge of the church.

The editor of *The Friend of Russia* wrote,

God's people can never get together on human creeds and disciplines. They are too narrow and changeable. We have a foundation that is broad enough to hold all. Christ Himself is this foundation. In Christ, all God's people are one, irrespective of race, color, social standing, or creed.

A certain preacher of standing in a prominent church outside the Pentecostal ranks, while addressing the baptized saints not long ago, said,

As we look upon the church divided, upon the sect-ridden multitude, none of whom can see alike, how our tried souls cry out for that original love. And we will never win the world on any other plane. It was said of the early Christians, by the heathen themselves, "Behold how these Christians love one another!" While we are breaking up into sects, creeds, isms, and doctrines, our love is dying. Our churches will be empty and our people lost. Your beautiful Pentecostal work, so full of promise, where God has designed to come in and fill souls and wonderfully baptize them in the Holy Spirit, is broken and peeled and ruined for lack of love.

Someone has recently written as follows:

It is a common thing to read in the daily papers such words as these: "Only union men need apply." And it is becoming a common thing to read in church papers: "Affiliating brethren are invited." What is the difference? No difference, except one is a secular union, the other is a religious union.

Every fresh division or party in the church gives the world a contradiction as to the oneness of the body of Christ and the truthfulness of the Gospel. Multitudes are bowing down and burning incense to a doctrine rather than Christ. The many sects in Christendom are, to say the least, evidence to the world that Christians cannot get along together. Written creeds only serve to publish the fact that we cannot understand the Word of God alike and get together on it. Is the Word of God, then, so hard to understand? They who establish a fixed creed bar the way to further progress.

It is said of the mighty evangelist, Charles G. Finney, that he "forged his theology on the anvil of prayer in his own heart." He was not bound by the systems of his day.

The Spirit is laboring for the unity of believers today—for the "one body"—so that the prayer of Jesus may be answered, *That they all may be one;...that the world may believe"* (John 17:21). But the saints are ever too ready to serve a system or party, to contend for religious, selfish, party interests. God's people are shut up in denominational coops. "Error always leads to militant exclusion. Truth evermore stoops to wash the saints' feet." *"By one Spirit are we all baptized into one body"* (1 Corinthians 12:13). We should be as one family, which we are, at home in God's house anywhere.

We belong to the whole body of Christ, both in heaven and on earth. God's church is one. It is a terrible thing to go about dismembering the body of Christ. How foolish and wicked the petty differences between Christians will appear in the light of eternity. Christ is the "issue," not some doctrine about Him. The Gospel leads to Him. It exalts Christ, not some particular doctrine. To know Christ is the alpha and the omega of the Christian faith and practice.

D'Aubigne, the historian, said, "The church was in the beginning a community of brethren guided by a few of the brethren." *"One is your Master, even Christ; and all ye are brethren"* (Matthew 23:8). We have too many who have a "leadership" spirit. These divide the body, separate the saints.

Now, however, we are coming around the circle, from the early church's fall, back to primitive love and unity, in the one body of Christ. This is doubtless the church for which Christ is coming, *"not having spot, or wrinkle, or any such thing"* (Ephesians 5:27).

Chapter 6

The Deeper Significance
of Pentecost

Frank Bartleman was a man of passion and deep burden. His prayers literally opened the heavens, and his messages were withering to all that was of the flesh. Everything that stood as an obstruction to the full exaltation of Jesus Christ as Lord of all became the object of his travailing prayer and was ruthlessly exposed by his fearless pen and tongue.

But Frank Bartleman was more than an intercessor and more than a dauntless revivalist. He was a man of vision—a prophet! He perceived the deeper significance of what the Holy Spirit was after in revival and called upon God's people to go on to that ultimate. His voice, although so long silent, now once again goes forth. The following message was *delivered in about 1925 shortly before Bartleman's death.*

The world is the field; the true church is the treasure—like a kernel in a shell. But the great nominal church, the ecclesiastical body in each generation, is also like a field in which the true spiritual church— the living church—like a treasure, is hidden.

But even this true, spiritual church is far from being the treasure of divine life and power originally planned and provided for in the purpose of God. Ever since the early church fell from New Testament purity and life, she has been like a backslider, fallen from the summit of apostolic days—though destined to return and yet enter into the full blessing of the Father's house.

I refer to the true, spiritual body of Christ. It is a prodigal son, wandered from the Father's house, but since the Reformation gradually returning. Nearly five centuries have now passed since the Reformation. The route back has been devious and long, with many a dark valley, as well as many a glorious summit. But steadily, relentlessly, the mighty Spirit of God has been moving on, restoring that which was lost and heading things up toward that great prophetic revelation of the body of Christ in unity and fullness—even one body, fully matured *"unto the measure of the stature of the fulness of Christ"* (Ephesians 4:13).

Beloved, unless we understand this, we will not be able to move on with God and understand the different stages, experiences, and various standards and operations in the church's history during this dispensation. That is why most Christians have failed to move on with God and to accept His cumulative unfoldings in the restoration of revelation, light, and experience, once lost, but now being restored to the true church.

If you do not fully see this, or if it seems to differ from your present idea of things, do bear with me. Before I am finished, I believe you will understand; and, if so, it may well transform your life, giving new and vital direction to your prayers and ministry.

The Heart of Our Trouble

The human soul is ever lazy toward God, and no one generation has seemed to be able to travel very far on its way back to God and His standard from which the early church fell. It is true that human error or understanding continually satisfies itself with a part instead of the whole, but the real fact is that men are not willing to pay the full price to come back fully to God's standard, to be all the Lord's.

The early church came forth from the Upper Room fresh in her *"first love"* (Revelation 2:4), baptized with the Holy Spirit, filled with God, possessing both the graces and gifts of the Spirit, and with a 100 percent consecration for God. This was the secret of her power. She was all for God, and God was all for her. This principle will apply in all ages, both individually and collectively. No sacrifice on the altar means no fire. The fire of God never falls on an empty altar. The greater the sacrifice, the more the fire.

When the prodigal gets home, and the church becomes 100 percent for God again, we will have the same power, the same life—and the same persecution from the world. The reason we have so little persecution now is that the Spirit cannot press the claims of God home on the world through us. When that happens, men must either surrender or fight.

"Jesus Christ, the same yesterday, and to day, and for ever" (Hebrews 13:8)! God never changes. We have changed. We are not waiting for God. God is waiting for us. The Holy Spirit is given; we are still in the dispensation opened on the Day of Pentecost. But God can only work when we are willing, yielded, and obedient. We tie God's hands.

The history of the church has been the same. Each company that has come forth in the line of restoration has run the same course. That is human, fallen nature. It is human failure, not God's. When everything dries up and dies out, we call upon God. This alone makes it possible for God to come. He must have some place to put His Spirit, and only empty vessels can be filled.

When we are filled with our own ways, think ourselves *"rich, and increased with goods"* spiritually (Revelation 3:17), God can give us nothing. *"To the hungry soul every bitter thing is sweet"* (Proverbs 27:7). The crumbs tasted good to the Syrophoenician woman, but well-fed children despise even dainties. (See Matthew 15:21–28.) They will throw the food across the table at one another. Like the children of Israel, they despise even *"angels' food"* (Psalm 78:23).

The best preacher in the land cannot preach with liberty when his message is not desired or received. The oil ceases to flow as soon as there are no more empty vessels to be filled. This will often explain why good preachers sometimes have liberty and at other times have no anointing. Criticism will stop the flow of oil through any preacher. Oil will not flow when frozen.

How It All Began

The early church ran well for a season. Everything went down before it. But by the third or fourth century, they had compromised to escape the cross. They sold out to the Devil, backslid, and went down into the Dark Ages. They lost the Holy Spirit anointing, the gifts, the life, the power, the joy, everything. The church became a prodigal, left the Father's house, and went to feeding swine.

The Devil found he could not stamp out the early church by killing them. For every one he killed, two sprang up. Like the children of Israel, *"the more they afflicted them, the more they multiplied and grew"* (Exodus 1:12). The early Christians vied with one another for a martyr's crown. They exposed themselves purposely, recklessly, for this reward. Someone has said the greatest call that ever came to man is the call to suffer in a noble cause.

Heaven was real to the early church—far more real than earth. In fact, they seem to have lived only for the next age. That was their longing, their goal, to be delivered from *"this present evil world"* (Galatians 1:4). It was the sole relief they looked forward to. This present life, after all, is the true saint's purgatory. It is the sinner's heaven—his only heaven—and that is sad beyond words to express! But, glory to God, it is our only hell! We are in the Enemy's country, running the gauntlet, with foes lined up on all sides—but we're just passing through.

Without question, it was God's desire to restore the backslidden, prodigal church at once, when she fell, just as He must have desired at once to restore the human race in the beginning, when they fell. But He could not. Human, fallen nature was too weak.

God also wanted to take the children of Israel right into Canaan from Kadesh-Barnea when He brought them out of Egypt. It was only a short journey, but they frustrated His purpose and desire. They grieved God and *"limited the Holy One of Israel"* (Psalm 78:41), just as it has ever been. In consequence, they stopped going forward, went to "milling around," and their *"carcases fell in the wilderness"* (Hebrews 3:17).

Beloved, whenever we stop going forward, we go to milling around. When an individual stops going forward for God, he begins to go in a circle, just as a man when lost in a forest ceases to go straight forward but wanders in a circle.

So it was with the early church. When they ceased to go forward, they started wandering in a circle and became lost in the Dark Ages. The Devil had found he could not destroy them or stop their march by persecuting and killing them; so he removed the cross, offering them titles, positions, honor, salaries, profits of every kind—and they fell for it.

They no longer needed to look to God for their protection and support. They were "like the nations round about them," just as the children of Israel when they rejected God as their King. (See Deuteronomy 17:14.) And so it is with our great church bodies of today. History repeats itself in every movement through human weakness and failure.

The Reformation and Subsequent History

Out of the Dark Ages came the great ecclesiastical, Roman hierarchy, which in time dominated the whole world, both political and religious. And the same condition has developed out of every fallen movement. An illegitimate, hybrid monster has come forth.

This was the condition of the formal church in Martin Luther's time. However, the living seed of the true church had remained buried in this mass, even through those long, dark centuries. This seed now began to spring up and germinate—the church within the church. The prodigal backslider began to come to himself at last and desire to return home. The church had fed on swine long enough!

Through the labors of such men as Huss, Wycliffe, Luther, Foxe, Wesley, Darby, Müller, Moody, Evan Roberts, Wigglesworth, and a host of others, the prodigal church has been coming home. But each company that God has been able to bring forth and give a fresh deposit of the Spirit and of the truth once lost, has sooner or later stopped short of the full goal. Although often gaining much ground and experiencing tremendous blessing, each group has ceased to go forward as a body and completely return to the early New Testament standard and realization.

Again and again the church climbed from the depths of some sectarian stranglehold, with its various stages of formalism and spiritual darkness, only to fall again, within perhaps only a generation, into sometimes an even worse state. Fortunately, each time, some new light and understanding of truth and God's ways were given upon which the next revival company could build. But in it all, it is the failure of man, not God's failure. Each company has only gone so far. It was certainly God's desire to fully restore the early church to her first estate and love at once, as it is true with every backslider. To think otherwise is to charge God with sin. But the church would not.

A backslider does not get back to God in a moment. He generally has more or less of a battle to get back, according to the light and experience that he has sinned against. The early church had great light and experience. If it were too easy to be fully restored, it would be too easy to backslide.

There is a natural law that is similar to this. Faith has been broken down. It is like a case of tuberculosis, where the tissues of the lungs have been destroyed. It is a hard fight back, even under favorable circumstances of rest and climate. To return to the "lowlands" generally means a return of the disease. So it is with the restored backslider. He must keep away from temptation ground and aggressively walk in obedience.

Today we can look back and see the different companies that, in the line of restoration, God has brought out in the church since the Middle Ages. We can see where they ceased to go forward with God, where they began to mill around in a circle, and where their carcasses fell in the wilderness as a body—Lutherans, Anglicans, Congregationalists, Methodists, the Salvation Army, and so forth. They ceased to be a forward company.

Whenever we cease to go forward and keep on the offensive for God, we stop and die as a people. In fact, a movement is no longer a movement when it stops moving—be it the Holiness Movement, the Pentecostal Movement, or any other movement. It may continue to increase both in numbers and in wealth, but that is not necessarily a sign of life and power with God. All anti-Christian movements can show that kind of growth. No movement has ever recovered itself, as a body, when it has once gone on the skids.

God's Movement

We do not have to leave movements. We simply move on with God! As long as a movement moves, we move with it. The different movements in the history of the church, although part of His true restoration, are only incidental with God. God has one great movement we should all belong to, and that has never ceased moving. It is God's move through the ages to redeem a fallen, lost world and carry that great blood-washed assembly on to His eternal purpose. It began when *"the Lamb* [was] *slain from the foundation of the world"* (Revelation 13:8) and will end when the last saint gets safely home to glory.

We must work for the kingdom of God as a whole, not for some pet individual party, organization, or movement. That has been the curse and cause of hindrance to our going on with God to full restoration in all generations. We have worshipped certain doctrines, party standards, partial experiences, and blessings, all fine as far as they go, but abnormal in themselves and only a part of the whole.

Most of these have been unbalanced, exaggerated misstatements of truth at best. In the end, they have generally brought bondage in place of blessing. They have broken fellowship, divided the children of God, and put the church in bondage to men and their ideas, standards, understandings, and opinions.

We must keep moving! The clearest light on truth and experience has not yet come. We still wait for the full restoration of the "pattern shown in the mount," that of the early New Testament apostolic church as a whole.

The great mistake has been to stop with sectarian, partial, abnormal revelations. We must keep our eyes on God, not on a party. Keep free from a party spirit. That is indicative of a respect of persons. Seek only God and His plan as a whole, His church as a whole.

Every company, in time, repeats the experience of the early church. They compromise to escape the cross and accept positions, salaries, titles, and ecclesiastical power. An ecclesiastical hierarchy arises, just as it did in the early church during the second and third centuries.

The backslidden church is still in an abnormal condition. It will continue to be so until it becomes fully restored to the first standard of apostolic Christianity from which it fell. No experience or revelation in the line of gradual restoration has been perfect in itself. All is abnormal, both in understanding and experience, until the perfect whole is realized and restored.

We need a readjustment of all our doctrines to the full, clear light of God in the Word. All past experiences must be examined and redefined in the light of the perfect whole.

Someone has said that every reformation is at its best and highest tide when it first comes forth. This would seem to be so, but at the same time the true church is ever moving on to maturity. I speak of the church within the church, the kernel in the shell, not the surrounding movement. Just as the individual believer who goes on with God gradually matures, so the church within the church is maturing toward the end of the age when she will be a full-grown church. The goal is not just the standard lost by the early church but that toward which they themselves were pressing—"a fully matured man," even *"the measure of the stature of the fulness of Christ"* (Ephesians 4:13).

Apostasy and Recovery

As with Israel in the Exodus, the *"mixed multitude"* (Exodus 12:38), the exterior shell of every movement with which it loads itself and in which it later becomes buried, falls to lusting for "flesh." One can usually judge the progress of this process by the things the movement comes to demand. Instead of delight in the pure Word, prayer and worship, a love for souls, and zeal for good works, there come entertainment, programs, musicals, sensationalism, and oratory. These things have no place in essential, true Christianity, but are professionalism—flesh! O God, deliver us from fleshly substitutes for the Spirit.

Most meetings can only be kept alive now by continuous entertainment, professional evangelism, and a strong social spirit. And this is all too true in Pentecostal, Holiness, and interdenominational circles, as well as in the older denominations. Where is the Life itself to draw the people and bring God to them as in the beginning? This is not New Testament. It is abnormal, grieving and limiting the Holy One of Israel in our midst.

Each movement seems to run its course faster than the one before it. Like the Niagara River, it flows downward more swiftly as it approaches the falls, the end of time. These are the last days of apostasy.

The fight gets harder as we get higher up in our restoration from the early church's fall. When Adam fell, the satanic powers intervened between the fallen race and God. God removed the seat of His presence with man from earth to heaven. So when the early church fell, she again lost the image of God that had, in a sense, been restored in New Testament days when the body of believers became the temple of the Holy Spirit. In a higher sense than Adam had known, the *spiritual wickedness in high places* (Ephesians 6:12) intervened between the church and God again. Now, the prodigal church, coming up out of the Dark Ages, has had to fight her way back through these evil powers. Each movement, as we go higher toward full restoration, has to meet a higher order of these wicked, spiritual powers and intelligences and hence must fight harder.

Each step forward necessarily requires a deeper preparation and greater spiritual equipment for a greater measure of restoration.

It was never God's decree that the experience of the church should be so long and drawn out in recovering the normal standard and going on to fullness. But we have ever sought to call our present abnormal understanding and experience normal. We must see that all has been abnormal since the early church's fall. Experiences, understanding—everything has been partial, unbalanced, and abnormal. Nothing has been perfectly understood, and all the different truths and experiences have only been parts of the whole.

We have not understood these truths and experiences, just as no machine is properly and clearly understood in detail except as we understand the whole. We have been recovering the whole in parts, without seeing the whole—thus we so often distort and over-emphasize the truth or experience that our particular movement has recovered. I trust you grasp this, for it is very important.

The New Testament church in the book of Acts entered normally into the fullness of the Spirit immediately at its inception, as for instance at Cornelius' household in the tenth chapter of Acts. The different phases of our salvation were all viewed as just so many parts of one glorious, normal whole. But all the various movements in the restoration, since the early reformers, have ceased in their turn to go forward to full realization. They have established their party standard of a partial, abnormal revelation, putting a part for the whole. Then, in human vanity, they have each contended they had it all.

This is sectarianism, and it is like a lot of dams holding back God's people from flowing on toward the vast ocean of God's fullness. God cares little for these partial standards of men—their names, sects or parties, slogans or standards. All is only partial, distorted light that finally becomes the enemy of the real truth as the Lord marches on to glory.

Each oncoming wave of the sea toward high tide must fight its way through the last receding one. So it is with the different movements toward a final restoration of the church. The immediately receding one especially hates and opposes the next oncoming one. What fools the Devil has made of us! Oh, that we might see it! However real and good, as far as they have gone, these past revivals and movements are each but faltering, uncertain steps toward the final goal.

Let's Go On!

God has but one church, whether in heaven where most of it is, or here on earth. And there is yet very much land to be possessed before we realize the divine purpose to which we are destined. We must recognize the whole body of Christ. In our human thoughts, we fail to recognize God when we meet Him. Those who dare to go further with God toward the full restoration are denounced and opposed by others as if they were of the Devil. And this was not just true of Luther and the Catholic Church—it was also true of Wesley and the Anglican Church, of Booth and the Methodist Church, and so on. And it is still true today. But, beloved, we must face it—the backslider has not yet been fully restored; the prodigal has not yet reached home. We must keep moving on!

Elijah's rain came out of a clear sky, without even the sign of a cloud to begin with—the result of faith alone. So the Pentecostal outpouring came in 1906. And this has been the case with every revival. Revival is the property of faith, not sight. There is nothing for sight to see in fallen nature but hopelessness. Revival and restoration must come from God, out of a clear sky. We are earthly and fleshly, but God is Spirit. God's Word is spirit and life (John 6:63), and faith in that Word brings the living God on the scene regardless of circumstances or outward prospects.

Will God visit His people again? Why not? As surely as He has done it in the past, He will do it again. God's skies are full of Pentecosts. He only waits for us to claim them. Do we not need one? Then we can have it, when we are willing to pay the price of obedient faith.

The church is not fully restored. No past group, after it has waned, has had the faith and vision to move God to visit them again. If they had, they would not be strewn along the way as more or less dead movements, their bones bleaching in the wilderness. None of them had future faith. They stopped short of the goal. None of them went clear through. They *"limited the Holy One of Israel"* (Psalm 78:41), just as we do today. They would not pay the price. That was the trouble. But worse than this, they justified themselves in their abnormal standards and opposed and condemned others who would go further. And still they do so.

The sin of the Jewish high church in Jesus' time was the same. They refused to go further themselves, and set themselves in their backslidden condition to oppose all who wished to go forward. That spelled their doom, and it will bring down the judgments of God on any denomination, movement, or group that follows in their steps.

But a Gideon's band is forming again today. Faith is rising. Another visitation from God is coming. It is only the Gideon's band that can ever bring or receive it—only a praying, consecrated, pilgrim band. They of the *"mixed multitude"* (Exodus 12:38) will not be in it, for they are too many and too fleshly. *"Upon man's flesh,"* the Lord said of the precious

143

anointing oil in the tabernacle, *"shall it not be poured"* (Exodus 30:32). God usually has to work with the little things, the weak things—the small, consecrated groups.

"I will pour water upon him that is thirsty, and floods upon the dry ground" (Isaiah 44:3). Dryness is a condition that invites rain. At such times men cry for rain. It is a cause for encouragement when we thirst for God. *"Blessed are they which do hunger and thirst ...for they shall be filled"* (Matthew 5:6). It was after an awful drought that Elijah's rain came. The rain is ready, beloved—when we want it, and when we are in a condition to receive it.

We must have the spirit of Caleb and Joshua, a different spirit from the multitude. They *"wholly followed the Lord"* (Numbers 32:12); therefore, they entered Canaan with the next company to go forward. They had their portion in it, while the old crowd died in the wilderness. No movement, as a movement, has ever gone all the way through to full restoration for the reasons I have explained. Hence, we must never become the property of, or limit ourselves to, a party or a movement. Worship only God. Join God in His great movement. Keep moving!

The End Is Nearing

We are rounding the corner toward complete recovery. God is again pressing His full claims upon His church and upon the world in this, the end of the age. But the Devil is also pressing his claims with great vigor. Whom will we serve? It is either 100 percent for God or for the Devil—there is no neutral ground. We are nearing the awesome climax of this deadly war between the kingdom of God and the kingdom of Satan. Each must be at his best for his side.

A normal church is always 100 percent for God. There can be no flirting with the Enemy. The church has no other business than to carry the Gospel to the world and press the claims of God upon His own. All its energies and resources should be used with that one object in view—*"Then shall the end come"* (Matthew 24:14). God waits for this.

Nothing but the zeal and the 100 percent consecration of the early church, both in laboring for the salvation of the nations and in building up the one true worldwide church, will or can satisfy God. He will accept no substitutes or compromise with our ideas and fleshly plans. There simply must be an utter abandonment to His full will and His great eternal purpose in His own children! Nothing short of this can clear our conscience and responsibility in the day of judgment. We could have done this long ago—if we had willed to do so—but we have not. Oh, let us not delay longer, but at once go right up and storm the Enemy's citadels, vowing never to withdraw our sword until Jesus comes and the whole land is ours!

We are rapidly approaching the last days. I am convinced that God is going to put the church through the fire to destroy the dross. Judgment begins at the house of God (1 Peter 4:17). And, believe me, nothing but 100 percent reality will remain! A theoretical salvation will not do.

We are reaching the culmination of this age, and nothing but a practical application of the Gospel can hope to survive. All else will be destroyed by the fires of worldwide persecution. God can only defend obedience to His Word. Never fear—He is going to have a church without spot or wrinkle (Ephesians 5:27). But do you and I want to have a part in it? A sectarian, competitive, selfish, self-seeking church cannot survive. The church must return to the spirit of the early church in the book of Acts. She must yield to God and press into His *"present truth"* (2 Peter 1:12) for this last hour—or perish in the fires of persecution and in her own blood. *"Our God is a consuming fire"* (Hebrews 12:29)!

Let us go on!

Special Epilogue

Revival and Recovery
by Arthur Wallis

Arthur Wallis, of Exeter, England, is a son of the late Captain Reginald Wallis and author of the well-known books, *In the Day of Thy Power* and *God's Chosen Fast*. This article is taken from a booklet entitled, "Revival and Reformation of the Church," which in cooperation with the author we have adapted and expanded.

It is one thing to be right with God and enjoy a real measure of personal communion with Him. It is quite another to understand His greater purposes and let our personal experience be properly related to that all-inclusive end. —John Myers, President
Voice Publications

"Remember not the former things nor consider the things of old. Behold, I am doing a new thing.

Now it springs forth, do you not perceive it?" (Isaiah 43:18–19 RSV).

In relation to this theme of revival and spiritual recovery, let us first survey the past, then view some of the significant trends of the present, and finally say a word about the prospects of the future.

The Past

If we are to understand what God is doing in these days—if we are to perceive His *"new thing"* for our day—we need to study the past. Not merely from history books, with their limited human viewpoint, but we must study history as we have light cast upon it by the Spirit through God's Holy Word.

Let us take a brief panoramic survey of the work of God's Spirit in the years that are past. As we scan the centuries, let us try to discover the principles on which God has been operating. What has He really been after during the years of the church's history? This is important, for what God is doing today can only be rightly understood as we grasp the pattern of what He has been doing down through the centuries.

Obviously, this is a large subject that could occupy volumes, but here we wish simply to point out what has been the master strategy behind the successive quickenings of the Spirit that have blessed the church in the past. In a word, we want to show that every wave of spiritual blessing has had in view not only the immediate renewal of spiritual life in that generation, but also the recovery of spiritual truth. That is, in all the great spiritual movements through the years, the Lord has been seeking to recover lost truth and bring His people back to original apostolic Christianity.

148

This reformation, or "recovery," aspect of God's moving through the centuries is unmistakable—and usually has been a balancing thrust in one or the other of two directions. Since truth and experience are inseparable and must be in balance if either is to reach its divine objective, we see the Lord moving to emphasize either doctrine and principle, or purity and fullness of life and power.

But whatever may be the emphasis or particular truth or phase of experience involved, in the mind and purpose of God there has always been but one final objective in view. That objective is a church—washed by the water of the Word of God (Ephesians 5:26)—that will fully experience and fully express Christ, not only in the earth, but also in the whole universe.

But let us go back and trace through history this principle in action.

The Early Church

In the New Testament we have a clear picture of the early church. It wasn't a perfect church because it was composed of human beings, and they are never perfect. However, the early church was perfect in constitution, perfect in the revelation of God's mind, received through His holy apostles and prophets. They had complete light and thus had no need to progress into fuller revelation in the ensuing centuries.

Through the apostles, the early church received in that first century a complete revelation of the mind of God. This revelation is, of course, contained in our New Testament. And, as they walked in the light of this revelation, not only the revelation but they themselves became a model of God's intention.

But alas, they did not always walk in the light that they had received, and things often went wrong. However, when this happened, the situation was dealt with in a way directed by God, and that also constitutes a pattern for restoration. Thus, not only in doctrine and principle, but also in practice, we have been given a perfect guide in the pages of the New Testament.

As the years went by, the church, which had been born in persecution, thrived in persecution. As with Israel of old, in bondage in Egypt, the more the church was persecuted the more she flourished and multiplied. The blood of the martyrs was then, and ever has been, the seed of the church.

The Fourth Century

Finding that this persecution was hastening God's purpose, the Devil changed his tactics. In the fourth century A.D., Constantine became the Roman emperor. He officially embraced Christianity. Whether he was genuinely converted to Christ is unknown, but nevertheless, Christianity became the legalized and accepted religion of the Roman Empire.

Instead of suffering the persecution of the state, the church now enjoyed the patronage of the state. She was taken off her guard. The people of God, who had been watchful, prayerful, and faithful in the time of opposition, were now lulled into a false sense of security.

Without doubt, imperial favor brought the world into the church, and what Satan had failed to do by persecution he achieved by patronage. As Dr. Edwin Orr has said, "It is one thing for the ship to be in the sea, but a different matter when the sea gets into the ship!" It is one thing for the church to be in the world, but when the world gets into the church a spiritual decline has set in.

Thus the "conversion" of Constantine, with the changes that this brought about—the introduction of practices of pagan origin, the rise of an ecclesiastical hierarchy based on the world system rather than Scriptures, and so on—led to a swift decline. The church descended into the dark Middle Ages, and the light of true Christianity was almost extinguished.

However, even through those dark centuries, as E. H. Broadbent shows in *The Pilgrim Church,* the light of testimony was kept burning here and there. A few men, like Francis of Assisi, arose as mighty giants of life and revelation, but the refreshing glow of their lives did not change the basic structure of things. There was no widespread movement, no general turning of the tide; and century after century, for a whole millennium, the tide of spiritual life continued to recede.

The Fourteenth Century

A thousand years from the time of Constantine brings us to the birth of a man destined to be one of the first great instruments in the turning of the tide. He was an Englishman, and his name was John Wycliffe. In the fourteenth century, England's only Bible was the Latin Vulgate. The common people, utterly ignorant of its contents, were living in abysmal spiritual darkness, until this brilliant Oxford scholar gave to England a version of God's Holy Word in the tongue of the common people.

This was God's first strategic move to bring back His church to New Testament faith and practice. A return to apostolic Christianity must of necessity be a return to the Word. Thus the foundation was laid. With Wycliffe there began that stirring of opposition to a church that had become so lifeless. A great preacher as well as a great scholar, Wycliffe soon made his voice heard. His position and influence gave him the ear of the people as he began to question the unscriptural practices of the church of that day. In the providence of God, a mighty wave of spiritual life began to roll in upon the shores of Christendom—the Recovery had begun!

The Fifteenth Century

Following Wycliffe, we have the spiritual movement known as the Lollards. They were the "poor priests" that Wycliffe sent out to take the simple message of the Gospel from place to place. They were humble itinerant preachers. And in the century following Wycliffe, so successful was this movement that at the height of its power 50 percent of the population of England were either Lollards or in sympathy with them—a remarkable movement of the Holy Spirit.

The preached Word, whatever its shortcomings may have been, contained the message of life, and hungry people received it. The Lollards were even more outspoken than Wycliffe. God was paving the way for the great movement that took place in the following century.

The Sixteenth Century

The sixteenth century saw the raising up of Martin Luther, John Calvin, and other great leaders. Under these Reformation giants, the church arose from its awful bondage, and set herself free from the ecclesiastical tyranny of centuries.

The glorious Reformation broke over Europe, bringing into clear light the great truth of justification by faith. People began to understand the genius of the Gospel of God's grace that had so long been obscured by a doctrine of salvation by works.

The work of reformation, however, was by no means complete. Although the reformed churches had abandoned much that was plainly contrary to Scripture, they still retained very much that was traditional—things that belonged more to the old order from which they had been delivered than to the New Testament Christianity toward which they were groping.

The Seventeenth Century

In the century following the Reformation, we have the great Puritan movement. God raised up expositors, men mighty in the Scriptures. They utilized and expanded the light that had come through the Reformation. The emphasis, of course, was on the importance of believers being well-grounded in the great doctrines of Scripture.

The hearts of God's people were expanding as God was giving them more truth, more light, and more understanding. More things that belonged to the past were put away, and earnest hearts began to grope forward again to a true position in the light of the teaching of God's Holy Word.

Out of the Puritan Revival came two strategic church movements that were significant developments in the move back to apostolic Christianity.

The Congregational Movement was a reaction against interference in the affairs of the local church from an ecclesiastical hierarchy. They had recovered the truth of the autonomy of each local church, its right to order its own affairs under the direct Headship of Christ.

The Baptist Movement, which was closely connected, also stood on this ground, while going a step further in emphasizing the truths involved in the believer's baptism by immersion.

The Eighteenth Century

The force of the Puritan Movement was spent as the eighteenth century dawned, and things seemed to be going from bad to worse. Too much emphasis on doctrine had no doubt caused a neglect of the "life" factor, and death was once again setting in. Religion was at a dangerously low ebb. Those who were supposed to be spiritual leaders had become corrupt and licentious; the common people were immoral and blasphemous.

It was then that God raised up two great men. They were Anglican clergymen; one, John Wesley, the other, George Whitefield. They were the two instruments in His hands for the great evangelical awakening that saved England from the horrors of the French Revolution.

The emphasis of the Methodist Revival, as it has sometimes been called, was at least threefold:

First, a bold assertion of instantaneous salvation by faith, accompanied by the inner witness, or assurance, of the Holy Spirit. This was followed, second, by a strong emphasis on the subjective side of the Christian life—holiness of heart and life. God was bringing His people back to the doctrine of heart purity and sanctity of walk. Third, there was the recovery of the truth—startling to the people of those days—that it was not necessary for a man to be formally educated and ordained to preach the Word. Any man who knew the commission of heaven could go forth as God's ambassador.

The requirement of a "consecrated building" in which to preach was also exposed as a dead tradition— why not preach in the open air as the Master did?

Thus Whitefield, Wesley, and their followers, under the open canopy of heaven, preached to vast throngs, and multitudes were swept into the kingdom. Another great step in the Recovery was consummated!

The Nineteenth Century

But by the turn of the next century this wave also had spent itself, and again the spiritual tide had receded. The need of revival was great. Here and there in the early part of the century there were stirrings and outpourings of the Spirit, but in 1858 God mightily poured out His Spirit in the United States, followed the next year by a similar outpouring in Ulster and in Wales almost simultaneously.

The revival in Ulster spread quickly to Scotland and soon was making its impact felt in different parts of England. God had again come in gracious power.

This century witnessed a number of significant movements in the great purpose of God to bring His people back to apostolic Christianity. One preceded the mid-century revival by a number of years; others were the products of it. How different these movements were, and yet each made its own contribution to the progress of spiritual recovery.

The first was the Brethren Movement, commencing about 1830, emphasizing the sufficiency and not merely the infallibility of the Book. They recovered the truth that the Bible reveals all that we need to know for both our daily walk and the ordering of our church affairs. They saw that the truth of the one body of Christ, as composed of all true believers, was the antidote to sectarianism. They also recovered the practical implications of the truth of the priesthood of all believers. Here was a serious attempt to return fully to New Testament Christianity.

Unlike many of the other recovery movements, the Brethren, to a very large extent, embraced all that had previously been recovered, besides adding the deeply significant points listed above.

However, again there came to be too much emphasis on doctrine, and out of the great revival of 1858 and 1859 there came further sweeping waves of refreshing heavenly life. These could be viewed as a divine reaction to the Brethren tendency to overemphasize objective teaching, thus supplementing the objective truth of what we are positionally, with the subjective truth of what we should be experientially.

The 1859 Revival in England brought a great wave of evangelistic fervor and missionary enterprise. Believers broke through denominational barriers and demonstrated in home evangelism and missionary outreach the oneness of the body that the Brethren were teaching.

In the midst of this wave of evangelism, the Salvation Army was born. A child of Methodism, the Salvation Army reemphasized Wesley's teaching on holiness and grasped what most of God's people had missed—the social implications of the Gospel. They had a concern for the underprivileged, the down-and-out, the underdog. With dauntless courage, heroic zeal, and challenging self-sacrifice, they preached the simple Gospel of God's grace and ministered to all who were in need.

Another wave of heavenly life focused on developing the great truths governing the personal victorious life, and especially the emphasis on the New Testament doctrine of the believer's union with Christ in His death and resurrection while the believer was still on this earth.

The Keswick Movement was no doubt the principal expression of this life-giving wave of blessing, as is expressed in the writings of Hannah Whitall Smith, Andrew Murray, Jesse Penn-Lewis, and a host of others.

Failure in Unity and Balance

Both this Keswick, inner-life emphasis, and the emphasis on the fervent preaching of the Gospel to all classes, with a practical ministry to the needy, were vital supplements to the waning Brethren Movement—though, sad to say, all these were never fully integrated.

As so often before, prejudice, sectarian pride, with its bondage to tradition, coupled with ignorance of the divine overall strategy, again prevailed to limit God and keep the one body of Christ broken up into variant doctrinal emphases and phases of Christian experience.

As expressed in the apostle Paul's heart-cry, *"Whether Paul, Apollos, or Cephas...all things are yours"* (1 Corinthians 3:22), God intended that all these waves of recovery blend together into one glorious whole with a balance of doctrinal truth and a dynamic spiritual life. Instead there was limitation of vision, each thinking that the part he held was the whole.

The Twentieth Century

The twentieth century commenced with a gracious movement of God's Spirit in the principality of Wales—the great 1904 Revival. Out of that revival came the worldwide Pentecostal Movement with its special emphasis upon the fullness of the Holy Spirit as a distinct experience, and its affirmation that the supernatural gifts of the Holy Spirit bestowed at Pentecost have never been permanently withdrawn from the church. This movement we could view as another supplementary reaction to the great recovery principles of the Brethren Movement.

Although orthodox in doctrine and successfully evangelistic from its inception, certain excesses and separatist tendencies in its early years alienated the Pentecostal Movement from the main body of evangelicals.

One regretful result of this alienation—strengthened greatly by the early Pentecostal tendency to substitute special enduement and revelation for thorough Bible study—has been a lack of the depth that characterized both the rich Keswick deeper-life teaching, as well as the Brethren emphasis on thorough Bible exposition, which had been carried over into general evangelical circles.

This lack of depth, however, had nothing to do with the basic doctrines of the movement. It was the natural result of separation from the deepening influences of the rest of the body of Christ.

It is true that a sort of Pentecostal pride—based on a sense of superior revelation and experience—played its part in the separation from other aspects of truth; but this also was not the fault of the new Recovery itself, but due rather to the Pentecostalist's application of the truth involved. Most reformation movements have had their share of this weakness.

It is necessary to stress this point, for it is still being much used by the Enemy to discredit what the Lord has done in this recovery wave, which is even now washing the shores of evangelical Christianity.

To illustrate this point: the Anglican Church was a product of the Reformation. The fact that it tends toward a ritualistic form of worship does not discredit the great Reformation principles that gave it birth and that are still enshrined in its charter, "The Thirty-nine Articles." There was a vital, even if only partial, recovery despite the atmosphere and accompaniments of its worship. These latter were a result of what they did not receive, and do not nullify what they did receive. Even so with the Pentecostal Movement.

At any rate, many of these excesses have been corrected, and thoughtful Christians who are not blinded by prejudice are coming to recognize increasingly that the Pentecostal Movement, in the providence of God, has come to make its special contribution to the great unfolding of God's truth.

It may be a surprise to some to know that the Pentecostals have the fastest expanding missionary movement in existence today. Their churches are springing up all over the world. One of their missionaries, associated with the founding of the Congo Evangelistic Mission, reports the establishing of a thousand assemblies of simple, baptized believers in the Congo. We cannot discount a movement that has been so manifestly blessed by God, though it may have been accompanied by blemishes—what movement has not?

Our Present Position

As we see what God has done in past centuries, it becomes obvious that we should not think that any movement has recovered everything, or has consummated the process. The attitude of "we have it all" has all too often characterized the more enlightened of God's people. In fact, the more light we have, the greater the danger of falling into this trap. This is spiritual pride and inevitably results in the halting of further spiritual progress. We must see each movement as part of a divinely instituted spiritual process that must go on until the consummation of the age. Our attitude should be that of John Robinson, who said in his farewell address to the Pilgrim fathers on their departure for New England in the *Mayflower,*

> If God reveals anything to you by another instrument, be as ready to receive it as ever you were to receive any truth by my ministry; for I am persuaded that the Lord has more truth yet to break forth out of His Holy Word.

In the midst of all the decay and confusion around us, both in the world and the church, may God help us to look heavenward and catch sight of His great purpose—even a church in the purity, power, and principles of New Testament Christianity!

When we turn from the church as we generally know it today and reexamine that stirring record of the early church, we seem to be in another world and to breathe another atmosphere. Does not the zeal, the courage, the power, the authority, the effectiveness, and the simplicity of those early Christians challenge us? What a long way we still have to go! Yet there are significant signs today that God is working—and Satan, too. Let us notice two significant trends.

The Movements toward Unity

The False: There is a trend that one feels to be dangerous. It has come to be known as the ecumenical movement, a movement toward unity among the churches. It is being hastened on by the threat of totalitarianism and an easy-going attitude toward biblical doctrine and practice.

Church leaders of differing communions are beginning to talk like this: "We may not agree about many things, but at least we must face the facts: totalitarianism and the cults are rapidly advancing in a world in which we make no progress. Let us sink our differences, emphasize the points on which we are agreed, and unite against the common foe. Unity is our only hope of survival."

Therefore, we are seeing a coming together of denominational leaders, the activity of the World Council of Churches, and other movements. The danger of this trend is that it is encouraging a unity that is based on compromise instead of conviction, a unity that is organizational instead of organic.

There is a spiritual unity, of course, that the New Testament teaches. We do not have to create it—God does that. We have only to preserve it. It is an organic unity, a unity of life, a unity of the Spirit that vitalizes the body.

This man-made organizational unity may well lead to what the Word of God predicts in Revelation 17, even a harlot church, that travesty of the pure virgin who is to be the bride of the Lamb. She is depicted as a woman riding a scarlet beast and is called *"BABYLON THE GREAT, THE MOTHER OF HARLOTS"* (Revelation 17:5).

Under the terrible pressures of the end times, with Christendom fighting for its existence, the meek and tolerant ecumenism of today could quickly harden into a religious despotism. A modern "Act of Uniformity" could force uncompromising evangelicals out of their churches. Apostate Christendom may then become again, as down the centuries, the greatest persecutor of the true body of Christ.

The True: God, however, has anticipated this stratagem of Satan. "Behold, I am doing a new thing. Will you not receive it?" (See Isaiah 43:19.) Yes, a new movement is under way. Though at present it appears to be divided into two distinct aspects, seemingly unconnected, it is in fact one move of God's Spirit in line with His principles of recovery.

First, He is stirring hearts all over the world with vision and faith for a true unity—even that spiritual unity of the one body of Christ—and at the same time He is also moving in nearly every circle of Christian life creating a thirst for Himself, for revival, for the Holy Spirit.

In regard to the aspect of the movement emphasizing spiritual unity, little needs to be said here. Like the Brethren Movement of old, the vision is the spiritual unity of the one body of Christ, encompassing all the various truths and experiences already recovered in past centuries.

Although still rather scattered and obviously in a formative stage, several amazing demonstrations of the strength of this movement are demanding the serious attention of the Christian world. Many firmly believe that it will not be too long before the eyes of thousands of restless, thirsty Christians the world over will be opened to see the significance of what God is doing, and a sweeping revival of New Testament Christianity will burst upon us.

Perhaps one of the important factors needed to detonate this glorious explosion is the blending of the two aspects of this movement. At any rate, let us consider the other aspect now.

The Thirst for the Spirit

"Blessed are they which do hunger and thirst...for they shall be filled" (Matthew 5:8).

This is exactly what God is doing today all over the Western world. He is filling His hungering and thirsting ones, as He said He would. Many are coming into a new experience of the Holy Spirit. They may have known His gracious work in their hearts and lives for years, but they have come to a strange state of spiritual dissatisfaction—a state surely created by the Spirit Himself.

These are beginning to long for something more than they have yet known. They notice that the early Christians knew a liberty, a joy, a power, an authority, a fruitfulness, and an effectiveness that seem in these days to be rarer than *"the gold of Ophir"* (Job 28:16). They say to themselves, "Why doesn't my experience at least approximate what these men knew in the Book? God hasn't changed, nor have the resources of the divine Spirit been expended. The difference must be in me, in my hardness of heart and my unbelief!"

Perhaps we have been brought up to believe that we had it all when we got converted. However, it is clear from the New Testament that the apostles and the early Christians did not have it all when they were converted. When we start to study this question in the Word with open minds and hearts, we discover that this being filled with the Holy Spirit of which the New Testament speaks is something definite and dynamic. It is something that makes a revolutionary difference in a person's life and witness. He knows when he has it, and very soon other people know also. How different this is from the rather vague and mystical thing that so many people think is being filled with the Spirit of God.

Dear reader, God wants to restore to the church all that she knew in New Testament times of His grace and His power. What we see in the New Testament is surely available to us. But are we open for it?

We may be interested in revival. We may believe that revival is the only hope of the church today. We may even be praying for it. But are we ready for what God may be about to do? Are we saying, "Lord, I want revival, but not revival with that"?

How would we feel if a gracious movement of the Holy Spirit should break out in our midst that was marked and accompanied by signs and wonders? What would we think if the Spirit of God was poured out as at the beginning, and there were tongues and prophecies and healing? "Oh, we want revival, Lord, but not that!"

Beloved, who are we to tell the Almighty how He should do His work? The sovereign Lord works as He will. Of course we must test the spirits. Of course we will want to be sure that what comes is truly from heaven. But we can be cautious without being critical. We can be discerning without being destructive. Oh, let us have an open mind lest we be among those who cling to tradition and miss God.

God is meeting with Christians today from churches and independent fellowships having no connection with the Pentecostal Movement. He is filling them with His Spirit as in apostolic times. Many testify to the transformation of life and service through the experience that God has given them.

We do not insist that supernatural signs are an essential ingredient of this fullness, but we are saying that God is sovereign. He works as He will, but we need to recognize the way He is working and be open and ready for Him to do what He will.

The Future

What does the future hold? We know it holds the blessed hope and glorious consummation of the age and the return of the Savior from heaven. But before that, the church should be prepared for two things: revival and persecution. As in apostolic times these two went together, so surely it will be in these end times. And to the prayerful and watchful, there are significant signs that both are on the way.

It is certain that at present we could not stand bitter or prolonged persecution. The church today would crack. It is only a revived, strong church that could be entrusted to withstand this fiery ordeal. Let us not hoodwink ourselves by thinking that it will never come to us—many of God's saints are going through it right now in countries under totalitarian rule.

Surely we must believe that God will revive us before we are called to go through the furnace of affliction. And believe me, brethren, in that hour we will need all the grace and depth of life and all the power and gifts of the Holy Spirit that God is willing to give.

One significant difference between the early church and the church today is this: they believed in the Holy Spirit while we are afraid of the Holy Spirit; they knew the Holy Spirit experientially while we so often know Him only theologically and theoretically. Will we at last let Him have His way? This is the pathway to revival.

Before closing may I ask, Is your life making an impact where God has put you? Are you a channel through which the rivers of living water are flowing day by day? If the answer is "No," are you willing for it to become true? Are you prepared to get on your knees and say, "Lord, whatever it may involve, make my life a channel for those rivers of living water! Continue to recover Your church, according to Your great purpose, and let me be a living part of that glorious recovery"?

On the far reef the breakers
Recoil in shattered foam,
Yet still the sea behind them
Urges its forces home;
Its chant of triumph surges
Through all the thunderous din—
The wave may break in failure,
But the tide is sure to win.

O mighty sea, thy message
In changing spray is cast:
Within God's plans of progress
It matters not at last
How wide the shores of evil,
How strong the reefs of sin—
The wave may be defeated,
But the tide is sure to win.

About the Author

B orn in a rural Pennsylvania town in 1871, Frank Bartleman grew up on his father's farm. His first job was to work the plow, though he suffered from relatively poor health all his life. He left home when he was seventeen and was converted in 1893, at the age of twenty-two, in the Grace Baptist Church of Philadelphia. Bartleman's desire to preach led him to enter full-time ministry the following summer. He was ordained by the Temple Baptist Church. Although he had the opportunity to be put through college and to one day have a paying position as a pastor, he chose instead "a humble walk of poverty and suffering," working in the streets and slums.

In 1897, the young minister left the Baptist ministry. He joined with the Holiness Movement and afterward spent some time with the Salvation Army, the Wesleyan Methodists, and the Peniel Missions. He rarely stayed at one address or in one church for very long. Bartleman's wandering lifestyle had a tendency to depress him, even to the point where he contemplated suicide in 1899. Yet he was not entirely despondent, for in 1900 he married Anna Ladd, the matron of a school for fallen girls in Pittsburgh, Pennsylvania.

Soon after he was married, Bartleman joined the Wesleyan Methodists and was assigned to a pastorate in Corry, Pennsylvania. Yet this ended up being a bad experience for him, as the church was far from moving toward an emotional and expressive Holiness religion, which was Bartleman's spiritual focus. So Bartleman headed west toward California, with his wife and the first of their four children, Esther, in tow.

In 1904, when the Bartlemans reached California, Frank was appointed as the director of the Peniel Mission, a Holiness rescue mission in the heart of Sacramento. From there he tried to reenter the church pastoral ministry, but when this failed he had to turn to odd jobs in order to keep his family alive. By December, he and his family had headed to Los Angeles, where hardship and tragedy awaited them. The death of their first child, Esther, in January 1905, threw him into a spell of grief; however, this loss ultimately caused him to strengthen his commitment to ministry.

Throughout 1905, Bartleman worked largely with the Holiness churches in Los Angeles, but he was always looking for the latest work of God. This led him to the Methodist and Baptist churches in the area, especially those connected with the revival going on in Wales at the time. For a time he supported the New Testament Church, pastored by Joseph Smale. He also attended the mission at Azusa Street and established another at Eighth and Maple Streets. Bartleman's wandering lifestyle as a young man had prepared him for following God's work throughout his life, for he preached as a traveling evangelist for forty-three years.

Bartleman's more than 550 articles, 100 tracts, and 6 books served as a complete and reliable record of the revival at Azusa Street and throughout Los Angeles from 1905 through 1911. Bartleman's reports were published and republished for holiness papers around the nation, and his reputation grew as a man who had a passion for increased unity and spiritual renewal among Pentecostals.

Frank Bartleman died on August 23, 1936, and is buried in Burbank, California.